Listening to
Life Stories

Bruce Rybarczyk, PhD, is a Clinical Psychologist and Assistant Professor at Rush Medical College and Rush-Presbyterian-St. Luke's Medical Center in Chicago. He has a joint appointment in the Departments of Psychology and Physical Medicine and Rehabilitation. He received his training at Virginia Commonwealth University and the Palo Alto VA Medical Center. His clinical and research interests include the complementary areas of behavioral medicine, geropsychology, and rehabilitation psychology. His research has focused on interventions and assessment techniques that address the overlap between mental and physical health, including the life narrative interview, a mind-body wellness program, and a psychotherapy approach for older adults with chronic illness. At the medical center, he teaches adult development, stress and coping, and patient interviewing to students and professionals from a variety of health care disciplines. He has an active outpatient psychotherapy practice and provides consultation services to a primary care medical office.

Albert Bellg, PhD, is an Assistant Professor at Rush Medical College and Rush-Presbyterian-St. Luke's Medical Center with joint appointments in the Departments of Psychology and Medicine. In addition to studying narrative approaches to stress management, he conducts clinical programs in preventive cardiology. His research interests include adult attachment and adjustment to illness, adherence to treatment, and doctor-patient relationships. He received his PhD in Clinical Psychology from the University of Rochester and was a Health Psychology Resident at Rush Medical Center. He was a Psychology Fellow in Consultation-Liaison Psychiatry at Henry Ford Hospital in Detroit, and a Fellow in the Advanced Clinical Educators' Fellowship in the Department of Medicine at the University of Rochester, where he studied doctor-patient communication. Prior to studying psychology, he had a 15-year career as a poet, public radio producer, essayist, creative writing teacher, and speechwriter.

Listening to Life Stories

A New Approach to Stress Intervention in Health Care

Bruce Rybarczyk, PhD
Albert Bellg, PhD

 Springer Publishing Company

Springer Publishing Company, Inc.
536 Broadway
New York, NY 10012-3955

Cover design by Margaret Dunin
Production Editor: Susan Gamer

97 98 99 00 / 5 4 3 2 1

Library of Congress Cataloging-in-Publication Data

Rybarczyk, Bruce.
    Listening to life stories : a new approach to stress intervention
in health care / Bruce Rybarczyk, Albert Bellg.
        p.   cm.
    Includes bibliographical references and index.
    ISBN 0-8261-9570-9
    1. Physician and patient.   2. Stress management. 3. Adjustment
(Psychology)   4. Patients—Counseling of.   5. Self-perception.
6. Self-efficacy.   7. Psychology—Biographical methods.
8. Reminiscing—Therapeutic use.   I. Bellg, Albert.   II. Title.
R727.3.R93   1997
610.69′6—dc21   96-48471
                                                                    CIP

Printed in the United States of America

This book is dedicated to our mothers, Constance and Mary,

who taught us a great deal about listening.

Contents

Foreword

"I would ask you to remember only this one thing," said Badger. "The stories people tell have a way of taking care of them. If stories come to you, care for them. And learn to give them away where they are needed. Sometimes a person needs a story more than food to stay alive."—Barry Lopez, Crow and Weasel

In a few hours [after being admitted to the hospital] Rusanov had lost his whole status in life, his honors, and his plans for the future, and had become 168 pounds of warm white flesh that did not know what would happen to it tomorrow.—Aleksandr Solzhenitsyn, The Cancer Ward

Health care today is rediscovering stories. For some decades, health professions have acted as if our sole salvation lay in science; the human aspects of care were a surface veneer, making the enterprise look prettier when present, but ultimately unnecessary for the real business at hand. We have slowly learned the error of this view. Too many patients in today's health system (like Rusanov in Solzhenitsyn's novel) receive technically adequate or even excellent care but suffer greatly because their basic human needs for meaning and connection remain unattended to. Moreover, health professionals are discovering increasingly that one cannot do biomedical work properly without caring for the patient as a person and forging an effective human relationship. Patients who feel cared for and listened to will reveal important details needed to reach an accurate diagnosis and will cooperate optimally in the resulting treatment plan.

We suffer when things happen to us which threaten our basic identity, our wholeness as persons. Often this happens at least in part because events don't make sense to us. The task of relieving suffering ultimately involves making sense of events, assigning a meaning to them. And the usual human way of doing this is to tell a story. We have some sense, even if unexpressed, of the unfolding stories of our lives. If we can tell a story about events that cause suffering, and the story situates these events meaningfully within our life narratives—so that we can see ourselves living through and past these events, and facing a future beyond them—then our suffering may be relieved, even when the underlying disease or symptom cannot be cured. These stories, moreover, may serve to reconnect us to our family or community, and to end the perceived isolation that usually accompanies suffering. In some instances it is no exaggeration to regard these stories of illness and suffering as lifesaving.

Doctors Rybarczyk and Bellg demonstrate for us one application of this renewed interest in stories. They show us how to use life narrative interviewing to reduce the stress of patients who are facing acute illness or invasive medical procedures. Their research has shown that this interviewing technique can easily be taught to volunteers as well as to health professionals; that it is quite effective in reducing stress, compared with other interventions; and that it produces a high level of satisfaction among the patients interviewed. These factors alone should commend this short and easily readable volume to those interested in improving the quality of health care, especially in hospitals.

Although they have demonstrated immediate improvement in coping and reduction in anxiety, Drs. Rybarczyk and Bellg are appropriately modest in the additional claims that they advance for this technique. They note, for instance, that they have yet to investigate long-term health benefits from these interview sessions. I would hope and indeed predict that future research will uncover some such effects. While it is overly simplistic to see a positive frame of mind as a magic bullet that will somehow vanquish all diseases, research shows that positive emotions, and especially a greater sense of control over one's life, can lead to improved health status in a number of ways. The Life Challenges Interview, designed especially to remind patients of their inner resources by means of which they have overcome past challenges, seems an excellent way to harness a sense of control over medical problems.

The authors also recommend modifications in this interview technique for physicians, who often have too little time scheduled with patients to employ the proposed 45- to 60-minute interview protocol. They note several medical situations where the technique may be especially helpful for physicians, even if of necessity administered in shorter bits over a series of visits. I would add one other suggestion for primary care physicians. A relatively small minority of patients return to their physicians relatively often with the same or similar symptoms and fail to respond to what appears to be the appropriate medical therapy. Many of these patients will end up having a specific form of psychological problem, often depression, at the bottom of this pattern; and so the physician must of course screen for such conditions. But if no obvious psychological diagnosis can be made, this might be an excellent opportunity to utilize the technique of life narrative interviewing, with a specific focus on past life challenges. As a result, the patient may appear to the physician for the first time as a fully rounded person (not as a bundle of complaints), and this enhanced relationship may lead to a much better therapeutic partnership in the future. Or the narrative may reveal new diagnostic clues that point to underlying psychological issues (or, on rare occasions, even an undiagnosed physical problem). I would predict with some confidence that the time devoted up front to these in-depth interviews will pay off over the long run in much less time wasted later on futile and frustrating symptom-oriented visits.

The technique of life narrative interviewing and related uses of narrative approaches to health care have many potential applications and benefits. I look forward to these authors' future work on ways to use the patient's story for enhanced healing.

Howard Brody, MD, PhD
Michigan State University

Howard Brody, MD, PhD, is Professor of Family Practice, Medical Humanities, and Philosophy at Michigan State University. He is also Director of the Center of Ethics and Humanities in the Life Sciences, and author of *Stories of Sickness* and *The Healer's Power.*

Preface

Our patients are continually trying to tell us stories about their lives. As health care professionals, our response typically runs the gamut from amusement to irritation, as we try to shift them to our clinical agenda. Yet the movement toward patient-centered and holistic approaches to health care has awakened in many of us an awareness that these personal stories are telling us something significant and that we ought to be paying attention to them. But we are not quite sure what to do when these moments come along. We don't know what clinical purpose the process of telling and listening to stories can serve.

In writing this book, we believe we are bringing good news to our fellow health care professionals. The news is simple: stories are important, they should be encouraged, and they can be used to help patients cope with stress. The goal of this book is to equip the reader with the knowledge to recognize these therapeutic opportunities and the skills necessary to guide the storytelling process so that patients are strengthened by their own stories.

The premise of our life narrative interview is that during times of stress, we need to be reminded of the positive aspects of our life, especially our strengths and resources. Being reminded serves as a short-term buffer against the feelings of vulnerability and helplessness that so often accompany medical illness and treatment. We have found that each individual, regardless of the misfortune in his or her life, has positive experiences that can be drawn upon for this purpose. We all have our high points, defining moments, and finest hours. This book emphasizes the skills necessary to keep the focus of the interview on these positive experiences.

The other key premise is that the listener has a key role in the storytelling process. In a very real sense, stories are "co-created" by teller and listener. The storyteller (the medical patient) constantly observes the listener (the medical caregiver) for subtle and not-so-subtle signs of interest and lack of interest, acceptance and nonacceptance. A responsive listener will inspire patients to tell meaningful stories and validate the personal attributes revealed in those stories.

An important agenda of this book is to empower health care professionals from all disciplines to be counselors to their stressed patients. Stress is a simple fact of the world of health care, whether that world is a hospital, an outpatient clinic, a nursing home, a hospice, or a dental office. Yet stress management is often viewed as the exclusive territory of mental health professionals, beyond the scope or training of other health professions. If other professionals do offer coping assistance to their patients, it is usually in the form of words of encouragement or a referral to a support group. We hope to convince readers that any of us can be more directly involved in managing stress by using the life narrative approach. Indeed, with the current emphasis in health care on reducing costs while improving quality of care, "cross training" in stress management is a timely idea.

While our research has focused on life narrative interventions in a 45-minute interview format, fortunately there are many other ways to use these techniques in shorter time periods. They can be worked into the fabric of our day-to-day conversations with patients, whenever and wherever there is an opportunity to listen to a story—and there are abundant opportunities. Life narrative interviews can be conducted while administering chemotherapy or obtaining a medical history, and even during a psychological counseling session. A series of brief "snapshot" stories shared over a period of time will accomplish many of the same objectives as a single longer interview.

We also wish to impress on readers that life stories serve a vital function whatever the age of the storyteller. Even though our research was initially directed toward older adults, the idea of using life narratives for stress intervention has been broadened to include individuals of all ages. We changed the name of the intervention from "reminiscence interview" to "life narrative interview" to reflect this shift. We find that reminiscing is too often regarded as an activity in which only older adults participate. That view does not do justice to the enormous psychological and interpersonal potential storytelling has for all individuals, regardless of age. We all need someone to bear witness to our unique journey in life, whatever its length has been.

Finally, we would like to encourage other investigators to explore the power of stories to promote coping. As Dr. Brody points out in the Foreword, there has been a surge of scholarly interest in the role of the patient's narrative in the illness experience. But this renewed interest has led to very little in the way of practical clinical research or guidelines on how to use stories in health care. We hope this book is a first step toward helping a wide variety of professionals apply this new understanding of narratives and storytelling to promote the well-being of patients.

The writer Elie Wiesel once quipped, "God created man because He loves a good story." We love a good story too, and our patients have some of the best stories around. Listening to them not only helps our patients but enriches our own lives.

Bruce Rybarczyk, PhD
Albert Bellg, PhD
October 6, 1996

Acknowledgments

My interest in life narratives grew out of a rich family tradition of story-telling, particularly by my two beloved grandmothers. This interest led to the idea of testing life narrative interviews as stress interventions for my doctoral dissertation in 1987. Steven Auerbach, my advisor, provided invaluable assistance in developing the idea and designing a research methodology. The Psychology Service at the McGuire VA Hospital provided a summer clerkship that supported the initial study. Later grants by the AARP Andrus Foundation and the American Cancer Society allowed the research program to continue. A series of research assistants made important contributions, including Michael Jorn, Marilyn Perlman, Ken Lofland, Julia Rahn, and Gail DeMarco. In addition, these studies could not have been conducted without the generous and enthusiastic contributions of a long line of volunteers. Special recognition goes to Bill, Jack, Woody, Joe, Ann, Lillian, Barbara, Martha, Lindy, and Diane.

I would like to express my deepest appreciation to the many patients who had the courage and trust to tell their stories to someone they had just met. Their inspiring stories made all the tedious work worthwhile. When we use segments of their interviews for illustration purposes, names and details have been changed to respect privacy. Likewise, the four case studies presented in the book are semifictitious composites of several different patients.

I've discovered that it takes a immense amount of support and assistance to write a book. To begin with, my brother Ken deserves much credit for helping to get the ball rolling. He was a superb writing coach and business advisor. Several other family members and colleagues made important contributions during the early stages of the manuscript, including my father, my sister Kathy, Lilian Schein, and Scott Terry. In the home stretch, there was a second group of readers who made valuable editorial comments: namely Martita Lopez (who also provided important advice on the first grant), William Tweedly, JoAnn O'Reilly, George Fitchett, Gary Schiro, and Marion Richeson. The staff at Springer, particularly Bill Tucker and Helvi Gold, provided a generous amount of guidance throughout the project. In the final weeks, Richard McKay came up with a terrific cover design. I also wish to thank my coauthor, Al, for taking the risk and joining me on this project when it was in need of a fresh perspective and new ideas. His expertise in storytelling, his writing skills, and his wisdom made for a perfect fit. Finally, thank you, Parke and Austin, for your abiding love and inspiration.

—B.R.

Most of my adult life, I have been listening to people's stories. I'm grateful to all the people who have shared their ideas and their lives with me and who have sustained my interest in storytelling both as an art and as a way of gaining insight and promoting personal change.

I particularly want to thank my coauthor, Bruce, for inviting me to be a part of this project. From our first phone conversation (which was long distance and lasted over an hour), it was clear that we had a lot to talk about. Furthermore, this book wouldn't exist without his research, which extends past work by others explaining what narratives do to show how they can be deliberately used to promote desirable outcomes in medical settings. He was a creative and inspiring collaborator, and great fun to work with.

Finally, I'd like to acknowledge the people who've supported me personally throughout the project: my colleagues at Rush; my mother and sister; my friends, particularly Steve and Beth (and Hope and Laurel); and Mary, who is a important part of my own story.

—A.B.

CHAPTER 1

An Introduction:
Storytelling in the Medical World

Patients are dying to tell you what's going on with them.
But we won't let them.—George Engel, M.D.

It's no great secret why we don't listen to patients' stories: we're busy. As medical caregivers of various sorts, we have information to gather, diagnoses to make, treatment plans to develop, medications to administer, therapy to conduct, and reports to write. But equally, it's no secret that as we get caught up in our professional role and duties, we often feel that we're missing something. We want more than our professional encounter with the patient. We want to connect with patients in a way that feels meaningful—to us and to them. We want to experience patients in a way that says something to both of us about the medical and human predicament in which they find themselves.

Interestingly, that experience is what patients want to share with us. As Dr. George Engel says (personal communication, 1992), they're just "dying" for someone to listen who isn't trying to get out of the room as soon as possible.

Robert M. was a 45-year-old man who had been diagnosed with a rare form of colon cancer 6 months earlier. He had been to a number of physicians and hospitals since that time, undergoing a variety of treatments, but the disease had gradually spread to his spine. Robert had been in our hospital for 1 month when he was referred to the psychosocial oncology service. His nurses identified him as needy and demanding, since he constantly seemed

1

to be requesting a drink of water, pain medication, or minor adjustments in his position in bed. Also, he wouldn't stop talking. Even his attending physician felt trapped and had difficulty extricating himself from the room without feeling that he was being rude. A nurse suggested with a smile that perhaps this was a job for someone trained in the "talking cure."

During our initial meeting, Robert was guarded. He didn't seem depressed, though he had moderate symptoms of anxiety. Beyond direct responses to questions, he didn't volunteer much information. It was during our second meeting that he started to talk—not about his illness or his pain but about himself.

He had accomplished a lot in, as he put it, his "fortunate life." He had served with distinction in the Vietnam War and was proud of his contribution. He had been the first in his family to get a college degree. He had eventually acquired a good union job with a manufacturing company maintaining and troubleshooting computer-controlled lathes. He had married, and he had a daughter, who was attending college at the time. He and his wife had a "solid" relationship and a home in the country that they both enjoyed greatly. His father had died of a heart attack when Robert was a teenager, but he still had a close relationship with his mother and two sisters.

The story Robert tells about his life is irrelevant, of course—that is, in terms of providing information to aid in his diagnosis or treatment. To judge his story by its biomedical or psychological utility, however, is to miss his point. He is telling his story (and hoping that it will be listened to) for a different reason.

Robert has a strong suspicion that his "fortunate life" is in jeopardy. And whether or not this is true, he is sure that he is not living the way he expected to. His sense of himself is eroding daily, as his illness and the medical treatments that enable him to stay alive overwhelm most of the simple pleasures and activities he took for granted less than a year before. As a result, he is losing his sense of who he is. Significantly, other people are also losing a sense of who he is. Robert no longer lives in a world where people are willing to accept him as the person he believes himself to be. He would like to be seen again as a unique person with a past as well as a present, a person defined by his life instead of his illness.

So Robert tells the story of the key accomplishments of his life. This is not only self-affirming but very daring in the medical setting, because in telling it he risks rejection or dismissal. As a storyteller, he places his life in the hands of the listener. Listening to his story with acceptance, interest, and even approval is more than an exercise: it is an acceptance of Robert himself. It is a way of seeing him the way he wants to be seen and of validating his life. Finally, it is also a way of entering into a relationship with him which he will value and which will allow him to share things that are truly important to him, including information that may be important to his medical care.

The purpose of this book is to examine the idea that personal stories told in stressful or life-threatening medical situations may help the storyteller cope with those situations and the stress they cause. However, by creating a better understanding of the storyteller as a person, these stories can also create a more satisfying relationship for the medical caregiver. In the care of patients with difficult or chronic medical conditions, it is common for professionals to feel frustrated, burned out, or demoralized. A more human relationship can serve to prevent these reactions. As Kleinman (1988) puts it, "Involvement with the biography of the sick person and interest in interpreting its relationship to the illness not infrequently will revivify the practitioner" (p. 237).

This book will provide medical caregivers with a practical process for listening to patients' stories. We describe two specific types of interviews that can be conducted, but similar techniques can be used in a variety of formal and informal situations, even in situations where there are constraints on the caregiver's time. In Robert's case, listening to his stories may have saved the caregiver a great deal of time. After several sessions, he was no longer reacting to his nurses and physicians in the needy and demanding way that had originally caused him to be referred.

TWO WAYS OF UNDERSTANDING

In the first session of a class on understanding the stories of medical patients, a slightly skeptical medical student noted that there is an old saying: "Don't let the truth get in the way of a good story." Indeed, there is a common perception that truth, or factual information, is to be found not in stories but through analytic and scientific ways of thinking. Many people in the scientific and medical communities assume, as this student assumed, that we may be seduced away from truth by the temptations of a good story and that storytelling itself is not to be trusted as a way of understanding.

Our own view, however, and that of many theorists and researchers, is that although storytelling is certainly different from analytic thinking, both processes are important and valid ways of representing the world, and neither is more "truthful" than the other. Jerome Bruner, for instance, has noted that these two ways of thinking—the narrative (or storytelling) mode and the propositional (or analytic) mode—are different ways of organizing experience (Bruner, 1986). As organizing

TABLE 1.1   Characteristics of Two Modes of Thinking

Narrative Mode	Analytic Mode
Concrete, sensory, imagistic	Abstract, conceptual
Personal active voice ("I did it")	Impersonal passive voice ("it was done")
Personal perspective ("my experience")	Impersonal perspective ("what happened")
Associative connections ("x happened, then y")	Logical, formal propositions ("x caused y to happen")
Subjective validity of information ("the way I saw it")	Objective validity of information ("the facts were . . . ")
Conscious and unconscious processing	Conscious processing

frameworks, they have different purposes, and it is important to determine which is most appropriate in a particular situation and context. Analytic reasoning is not relevant to understanding every aspect of a medical situation, and neither is narrative processing.

Although the narrative and analytical processes can be complementary (as in the use of medical case studies to illustrate general disease or treatment principles), they differ substantially (these differences are summarized in Table 1.1). The most important distinctions for our purposes are how the narrative mode of thinking affects the creation of (1) meaning, (2) identity, and (3) relationship with others.

Both analytic and narrative processes are inspired by a need for understanding, or *meaning*. Analytic meaning is created by faithful adherence to the logical or scientific process, which then imbues the results with validity and scientific significance (though not necessarily clinical or personal significance; it's an old joke that scientific results may be "significant but not important"). In contrast, narrative meaning is distinctly personal and is created by the storyteller's construction of events, characters, and actions within the overall story. For instance—even though this was not explicitly stated—Robert's story about his father's early death figured prominently in the rest of his life story because Robert was seeing that event as a sign that he too might die at an early age. This part of his story helps explain Robert's reaction to the news that his disease was getting worse.

Along with personal meaning, stories also convey cultural meaning in the form of values, ideas, and feelings. We all belong to many cultures. Stories that are part of our civic culture (e.g., the events of the civil rights movement of the 1950s and 1960s) influence how we understand ourselves as citizens of a nation and of the world. Stories from our religious culture (e.g., stories about Jesus or the Buddha) convey religious and moral values and give us a context for our religious beliefs. Our individual family cultures, in the form of our family stories, strongly influence how we understand ourselves and provide models for how to relate to others. Finally, the stories we tell in our medical culture (e.g., about the struggle to conquer disease or alleviate suffering) define the meaning of our actions as medical caregivers.

The stories that patients tell also represent their sense of *identity*. This is seen in the way they characterize themselves in their stories, both directly ("I was proud of my years in the service") and indirectly ("Painful things happened to me that I survived"). For instance, Robert's stories were about himself as an independent, strong, generous person, although it is clear that his illness was causing him to doubt this characterization of himself. Robert was facing a medical and social situation in which he had little control over simple things that he had taken for granted, such as being free of pain and being able to go to the bathroom when he wanted. Telling his personal stories was partly a way of looking for affirmation that he was still the same person.

We have heard other patients tell stories in which they indirectly describe themselves as victims of circumstance or bad luck, or as surrounded by untrustworthy people who are out to take advantage of them. Listening to such stories with care and empathy makes it possible for the storyteller to feel affirmed at least as a survivor of such circumstances. The caregiver can also address any feelings of helplessness or mistrust. The interviews described in this book, however, ask the patient to shift the focus from negative to positive stories. These stories are enjoyable to tell and give the listener an opportunity to reinforce the storyteller's positive character traits.

Stories also give us a vivid picture of the storyteller's *relationship* with the listener. Although not everyone will hear (or needs to hear) every story the patient tells, the stories that caregivers hear will be in part a measure of how receptive, nonjudgmental, and understanding the listener is perceived to be—at least as far as these experiences are concerned. Sadly, in medical settings, the stories that patients tell often represent the distance they feel from their caregivers or the limitations they experience in those relationships. This is often represented indirectly by what patients leave out of their stories. For example, most patients have learned through past experience that their physicians are busy and pressed for time, so they usually confine their stories to the medical symptoms they know the physicians want to hear, leaving out most of their personal issues and experiences. Also, patients are often apprehensive about describing their difficulties in handling an illness, because they may be seen as "crazy." Willingness to listen to patients and encourage them to tell more of what's important to them can open up new possibilities in their relationships with caregivers.

In sum, storytelling is the creation of personal meaning, identity, and relationship. It is a way of representing reality, the storyteller's understanding of his or her place in that reality, and the role others play in it. More specifically, the way we listen and respond to the life stories of medical patients can have a profound effect on patients' understanding of their illnesses, themselves, and their caregivers. Positive experiences of storytelling, even if such an experience is brief, help establish empathy, rapport, and understanding between caregiver and patient and create a richly human context for working together on the patient's medical and personal difficulties.

STORIES ABOUT ILLNESS, SUFFERING, AND COPING

Illness is as an assault on our sense of self, and therefore it underscores our need to say who we are. Medical patients use stories not only to tell about their symptoms and their treatment but to convey their attitudes and feelings about their illness. In essence, they are conveying who they are through their responses to their illness. In their stories, they create a kind of map of themselves in their world, defining the points in their lives where they can and cannot handle things, where the illness is and where it isn't, where they are frightened and where they are confident, where they are still strong and where they have become weak. Kleinman (1988) calls these stories "illness narratives."

In providing an orientation to their disease, their prognosis, and their mortality, and in establishing a supportive relationship with the listener, stories help patients cope with suffering. Suffering takes place when people experience a threat to their identity or the potential destruction of an important aspect of self (Cassell, 1991). Suffering can occur in relation to any aspect of the person, including a threat to his or her loved ones. It also occurs as a result not so much of the physical experience a person is having but rather of what he or she understands that experience to mean.

For instance, a wide variety of experiences are associated with breast cancer and its treatment. Many women report that the worst experience, worse even than hearing the diagnosis or undergoing a mastectomy, is the loss of their hair following chemotherapy. Hair is a part of their identity that has great importance to them, and losing it is the most public, most revealing announcement of their illness. Of course, not every woman feels this way. Each woman has her own sense and interpretation of the issues and experiences that are closest to the core of her being and that threaten her sense of self.

Experiences that threaten one's sense of self may be a result of not understanding the cause of a particular symptom and assuming the worst. Or they may result from a lack of control over pain, nausea, or other symptoms, when these symptoms are overwhelming in magnitude or duration. Suffering also comes from vague or specific fears about what might happen down the road, such as loss of physical abilities, abandonment by friends or family, or some type of physical mutilation. In addition, suffering occurs when there is a breakdown in empathic and caring support. For instance, suffering can occur when a patient's caregivers doubt or minimize his or her symptoms. It can occur when an illness threatens personal and work relationships and the patient's roles in the lives of family and friends.

However, not every health problem is a threat to personhood; in fact, it is clear that suffering is as individual as a fingerprint. This is one of the reasons why each patient's story is different. Not only is the actual raw material of each person's illness and life different, but the way patients use a story may be unique to their way of coping with illness. They may also look for a story from their caregiver that will allow them to see symptoms as less distressing (for instance, a story about how another patient with the same diagnosis made it back to work within 2 weeks of surgery). Or they may use stories to give themselves a sense of control over how much their illness intrudes into their lives (for instance, a story distinguishing between aspects of life that are and are not substantially affected by their illness). A story may also be used by the patient to let others know about a particular aspect of self that may be threatened by the illness and that needs the support of an empathic listener.

So illness stories and life stories in the medical context have multiple functions. Patients want to tell their stories because storytelling is a natural part of being human. Humans sat around the fire for millennia sharing details of the hunt, discussing relationships within the tribe, and marveling at how they survived a terrible dry season years ago. It is not surprising, therefore, that medical patients use stories spontaneously and naturally as a way to cope with illness, creating a context for understanding the experience of illness and even for transcending the emotional and physical hardships caused by the illness. By encouraging and listening to these stories, we can help alleviate suffering.

THE HEALTH PROFESSIONAL'S PERSPECTIVE AND THE PATIENT'S STORY

As most of us have experienced, medical caregivers have a special relationship with patients. Physicians, nurses, psychologists, social workers, chaplains, and even hospital volunteers take on important roles in the minds of patients. These roles become part of patients' stories about their illnesses. From both the caregiver's and the patient's perspective, this relationship can be deeply satisfying or highly problematic, but either way it has implications for the interaction between storyteller and listener.

Patients assume (not always correctly) that a caregiver knows more than they do about what's going on with them. They look to the caregiver—to us—to find out what is important and what is not, what they need to pay attention to and what they can ignore. They also look to us, rightly or wrongly, for a sense of control over what is happening to them, as well as for the reassurance that comes from having a sense of control. Patients may also look to us for emotional support, and even for a scapegoat if things are going wrong.

A potential difficulty comes, however, when we are not attuned to differences between a patient's story and our own perspective on his or her illness. Such differences can arise in at least three ways. First, there is the specialized language that we use—the language that is most meaningful to us as professionals, the "voice of medicine" as opposed to the "voice of the lifeworld" (Mishler, 1984). It is with this language, from our various professional perspectives, that we go about our business of identifying and combating disease, caring for patients' physical needs, and minimizing their emotional distress. Second, we also have our personal and professional perspectives on "good" and "bad" patients, on "easy" situations and "hard" struggles. Third, all of us have our own perspectives on our purpose in caring for others: to conquer disease, rescue people in trouble, repay the world for a gift we've been given, or pursue a spiritual mission.

To say that we have our own needs and that we meet these needs through our work is not to denigrate or minimize the work. What it does mean, however, is that although we may be interacting with our patients on a daily basis or even a moment-to-moment basis, we may not be attuned to the stories that they are living. A patient may be looking for emotional support, but from a "diagnose and treat" perspective, we may miss that need completely. Or a patient may be looking for relief of pain, but finding no physiological basis for the pain, we may suspect him or her of being addicted to painkillers and may thus withhold medical and personal support in a way that increases the patient's suffering.

Helen R. was a 61-year-old married woman admitted for inpatient physical rehabilitation with a diagnosis of postpolio syndrome. After a week on the unit, she started to criticize some staff members for not being fully informed about this new condition. She had put much time and effort into educating herself about the syndrome through literature obtained from the national polio association. Helen's behavior either puzzled or angered staff members. She was labeled a "difficult" patient who should be discharged as soon as possible.

When Helen finally shared her story with a staff member, it explained a great deal. The main theme of her life story was the efforts she had to make to overcome various barriers. After she contracted polio as a child, Chicago public school officials insisted that she attend a special vocational school for handicapped children. Her blue-collar parents refused to go along with this and had to go to court to get her into a "mainstream" school. A few years later, they had to travel out of state to find a surgeon to perform a procedure that would help her walk better. Doctors in Chicago had insisted that the surgery would be risky and even if successful, would provide little benefit. A similar situation occurred later in her life, when she decided to go to night school to become an accountant while working full-time as a secretary. Several family members and friends discouraged her, saying that it would be difficult for her to marry and raise a family. As it turned out, Helen was able to do both very well.

Unfortunately, Helen was forced to retire early from her successful career because of fatigue and problems with mobility. She and her husband had been planning not to retire until age 65, at which time they were going to move to Arizona. She had also planned to take up horseback riding, which was a lifelong passion of her favorite uncle. In spite of her caregivers' views to the contrary, she believed that unless her physicians could find a treatment, she would have very difficult years ahead.

It's clear that the perspective we have about helping may be different from the patient's. For instance, in Helen's case there were several differences in viewpoint that needed to be taken into account. Our work with patients can be disrupted by assumptions we make about our role, the language we use, the amount of time available to spend with them, and the physical geography of the space in which we interact. All of these factors have been discussed in great detail by other writers. What is important is to acknowledge the differences between the medical culture and the patient's culture and to work to establish an empathic storytelling connection that can bridge the gap between these two worlds.

NARRATIVE INTERVENTIONS IN THE MEDICAL CONTEXT

This book will present a new approach to stress intervention in health care, based on the stories that patients tell about their lives. We call the process of asking about and listening to those stories *life narrative interviewing.* But before we go on to discuss how caregivers can use the storytelling-listening process to facilitate patients' coping, it is worth making two distinctions about what the process of listening to stories is and what it is not.

It's not psychotherapy, for one thing. Although therapy is based on a similar empathic relationship, most therapy with medical patients will deal *directly* with the patients' current experience of their illness, identifying problems and pursuing positive changes in the patients' psychological state or coping style. Nor do life narrative interviews provide medical information to patients about their illnesses; this information is more appropriately a part of other interactions between the patient and the medical staff.

Although they are not therapy, the interviews described in this book are designed to have a significant positive effect on the way patients cope and on their level of anxiety and distress. The interviews assume that empathic relationships are potentially powerful and do not need to be called "therapy" in order to have an impact. It may be most appropriate to think of these life narrative interviews as a way of being therapeutic without being a therapist.

To summarize, life narrative interviews are interactions in which the patient is encouraged to tell stories about his or her life. The goal of the interview is to affirm the storyteller's sense of self, promote positive relationships within the medical setting, reinforce positive coping strategies, and counteract the negative moods created by stress. The life narrative interview may be set up as a formal event or may occur informally as part of other medical caregiving. In either case, the interviewer's task is more difficult than it may seem. It requires the interviewer to listen and interact in such a way that the storyteller is able to talk easily and comfortably about positive life experiences. The primary objective of this book is to equip the medical caregiver for this task.

REFERENCES

Bruner, J. S. (1986). *Actual minds, possible worlds.* Cambridge, MA: Harvard University Press.

Cassell, E. J. (1991). *The nature of suffering: And the goals of medicine.* New York: Oxford University Press.

Kleinman, A. (1988). *The illness narratives: Suffering, healing, and the human condition.* New York: Basic Books.

Mishler (1984). *The discourse of medicine: Dialectics of medical interviews.* Norwood, NJ: Ablex.

CHAPTER 2

Using Life Narratives to Enhance Coping

It is an inescapable fact about human existence that we are made of our memories: we are what we remember ourselves to be.
—*E. S. Casey* (Remembering: A Phenomenological Study)

The central thesis of this book is that by inviting patients to tell their stories, we can empower them to cope more effectively with the stress they are facing. We are specifically interested in the stories that make up an individual's life story, or life narrative. Gerontologists have written extensively about reminiscing, providing much insight into the process of storytelling about personal experience. Thus we will begin this chapter with a section reviewing the different forms and functions of reminiscence. The next two sections will review two approaches to psychological intervention that center on storytelling about the past: reminiscence therapy and narrative therapy. Both of these approaches have influenced the development of the interview techniques presented in this book.

TYPES OF REMINISCENCE

During the past 30 years, there has been a growing interest in the meaning and function of recalling past events, privately or in conversation.

13

Yet before a groundbreaking article by Butler in 1963, very little was known about this subject. There had been a few observations about the tendency of older adults to talk about the past, but this commentary took a distinctly negative view: reminiscence was seen as a sign of senility or of living in the past. A positive view of reminiscence began to emerge in the 1970s, with the growth of gerontology as a discipline and with an overall cultural shift toward a greater appreciation of our individual roots. More recently, with the increasing popularity of oral history and genealogy, more Americans are seeing the elderly as a rich source of information about social history and family heritage.

The study of reminiscence has now expanded to include a wide spectrum of activities that serve diverse social and psychological purposes. Although most of the writing on the subject addresses older adults, the limited research that has been done shows that reminiscing is important during all stages of the life span (Webster, 1995). Contrary to popular belief, reminiscing is not more frequent in old age (Hyland & Ackerman, 1988; Merriam & Cross, 1982; Romaniuk & Romaniuk, 1983; Webster, 1994). Our own point of view is that storytelling about the past is an essential psychological task that can enhance coping for patients *of all ages.*

Researchers have developed several taxonomies to classify the forms and functions of reminiscence (Coleman, 1974; LoGerfo, 1980; Priefer & Gambert, 1984, Wong & Watt, 1991). By identifying different types of reminiscence, interviewers can more easily distinguish between narrative processes that are constructive and those that detract from the purpose of the life narrative interview.

We will present a composite set of five categories of reminiscence, covering those that occur most often in the storytelling-listening context (see Table 2.1). In focusing on the storytelling context, we omit the other types of reminiscing that occur in private thought or autobiographical writing, which are beyond the scope of an interview.

Category 1, *simple reminiscence,* is the most common form (Coleman) and the type most often elicited in life narrative interviews. It is recognized by its simple purpose: to evoke positive feelings in both the storyteller and the listener. It has two subtypes: generational and personal.

Simple *generational* reminiscence involves the vivid recall of a historical event (e.g., "I remember when computers first came on the scene. They seemed so complicated and cumbersome"). This version of simple reminiscing is often undertaken to find a common ground of positive feelings between two individuals in the same age group. When two middle-aged men discuss the 1968 World Series, for example, they are evoking

TABLE 2.1   Categories and Subtypes of Interpersonal Reminiscence

1. Simple reminiscence
    Generational
    Personal
2. Mastery reminiscence
3. Integrative reminiscence
    Life Review
4. Transmissive reminiscence
5. Negative reminiscence
    Obsessive
    Escapist

the thrills and excitement they both experienced at the time and are creating an emotional connection. However, simple generational reminiscing can also be used to bridge the gap between individuals from two age groups—for example, by letting the younger person in on what it was like to "be there."

Simple *personal* reminiscence serves the same function—eliciting positive feelings—but also has a secondary benefit: communicating to others *who we are*. Take, for instance, the case of an arthritis patient who tells a nurse a funny and engaging story about the first movie she attended as a teenager. By emphasizing how she skipped school to go to the movie, she is conveying her self-perception as someone who is carefree and has a taste for adventure. In addition, she may be communicating indirectly to the nurse that while it seems as if all her time is consumed with the tedious tasks of managing her illness, that is not who she really is at heart.

Each person has a vast reservoir of remote memories that can be shared with others to elicit positive feelings. Even nostalgia—a semisorrowful feeling—is usually experienced as pleasant. The natural "high" that comes from rose-colored memories is intensified when it is shared with an audience. As a demonstration of these mood-elevating effects, Fallot (1980) had volunteers conduct 45-minute interviews with older adults they had just met, asking them to "tell their life story." These interviews resulted in significantly more positive mood changes than interviews where subjects were asked to talk about present interests and activities. This was one of the first indications from research that simple reminiscence could function to counteract stress-induced anxiety.

Category 2, *mastery reminiscence,* is central to coping and life narrative interviewing. Mastery reminiscence serves the twofold purpose of reinforcing our sense of mastery and empowering us to cope with present and future challenges. This type of reminiscence recalls past accomplishments and triumphs over adversity (e.g., doing well in school, getting a first job, surviving the blizzard of 1977) which in turn serve as reminders of individual competence and resources (Brink, 1979). Wong (1995) provided a typical example of category 2: "Ever since I was a child, I always dreamed about becoming a nurse. I had to work several years to save up money and I had to talk to my parents on several occasions until they finally agreed to let me leave home and move to the city to study nursing. But I'll tell you, it was worth it" (p. 25). This type of reminiscing usually occurs within the context of simple reminiscing.

According to self-efficacy theory, the degree to which individuals are able to complete a task or cope with adversity depends to a large extent on their beliefs regarding their coping skills (Bandura, 1986). Thus individuals who are able to recall and rehearse past episodes of successful coping should have higher levels of self-efficacy. Although research is limited, one study reported a link between reminiscing about past coping experiences and "successful aging" (Wong & Watt, 1991); another study showed that overall frequency of reminiscing was related to adjustment to relocation (C. N. Lewis, 1971); and a survey found that one third of older adults reported using reminiscence to cope with current problems (Romaniuk & Romaniuk, 1981). It seems logical to assume that an intervention which promotes mastery reminiscence would facilitate this natural coping process; and this rationale is the basis for the "life challenges" interview in Chapter 7.

Category 3, *integrative reminiscence,* serves the vital psychological function of finding meaning in our lives and achieving a sense of continuity between past and present (Wong & Watt, 1991). Telling stories to others about past events provides an opportunity to edit these events so that they appear meaningful and consistent within the bigger picture of a life story. Wong (1995) provides an example of an integrative reminiscence reconciling an early ambition with an eventual career: "I always wanted to be a writer, but I discovered that I just don't have the talent, so I became an editor" (p. 24).

Although recent research has found that reminiscence is important to people of all ages, integrative reminiscence plays a uniquely important role in late adulthood. One of the most overlooked facts about old age is the preeminence of past experiences in determining identity: "I am who

I was." In old age, the process of "constructing a life story and recon-structing the self in that story" is perhaps the most important psycho-logical task (Sherman, 1991). At least one gerontologist has observed that this process is more important to life satisfaction in late adulthood than more current interests and activities (Kaufman, 1986).

During major life crises, such as transitions, losses, and illness, inte-grative reminiscence appears to be essential to preserving a sense of continuity of self. At these critical junctures in life, connecting the pre-sent self to the past self is an important part of the coping process. The geropsychologist David Gutmann explains this particular function of rem-iniscence for older adults: "Through reminiscence, older persons may creatively revise their past to conform to some sustaining personal myth; by finding or constructing the threads that connect the current self with some past, idealized self, they can overcome the devastating experience of discontinuity and self-alienation" (1990, p. 43). Although the research is limited (Havinghurst & Glasser, 1972), clinicians have noted that the quantity of integrative reminiscing increases during transitions, bereave-ment, and medical setbacks (e.g., hospitalization). Integrative reminis-cence occurs sporadically during life narrative interviews and should be encouraged.

The gerontological literature also makes frequent reference to a sub-type of integrative reminiscence, a more narrow version called *life review*. Butler (1963) coined this term to refer to the process of "putting the past in order." Specifically, he viewed life review as universal in late adulthood and as triggered by a heightened awareness of impending death. The life review process, which occurs both privately and in con-versation, involves a searching and analytical review of the choices made in life (e.g., why one decided to remain single or change careers in midlife). The emphasis is on coming to terms with choices as well as missed opportunities, unresolved conflicts, and past defeats.

An example of life review recently occurred in a psychotherapy ses-sion conducted by one of the authors with a 72-year-old woman. She had made a decision as a young woman that she would never travel by air-plane, after a frightening experience during her first and only flight, when she was pregnant. Later in life, as her children and grandchildren relo-cated to different cities and states, this choice made it necessary for her to use other modes of transportation, mainly cars and trains. She recounted that she saw her family less often, but for longer periods of time. Likewise, she talked at length about the advantages of all her car and train travel. The therapy session gave her an opportunity to work through these issues and receive some validation for her feelings.

The concept of life review has been linked to Erik Erikson's (1950) popular stage theory of psychosocial development, which holds that the final developmental task of life is the achievement of ego integrity. Ego integrity occurs when a person reaches the point of seeing "one's one and only life cycle as something that had to be and by necessity permitted no substitution." As noted in the next section, this theory of life review has led to a set of psychotherapy techniques that attempt to facilitate the process. However, since this type of reminiscing deals with unresolved issues that take time to work through, it should be avoided in a life narrative interview.

Category 4, *transmissive reminiscence,* is another form of reminiscence that should be downplayed in a life narrative interview. This type of reminiscing involves recounting past events for the purpose of teaching a lesson to younger generations (Wong & Watt, 1991): "When I was your age, I had to get up at sunrise to do several hours of chores and then walked 5 miles to school. I was allowed to go to school only until I was 14." This type of story carries a lesson or moral, such as "Education is important and should be considered a privilege." The storyteller also obtains psychological benefits—respect, for instance—from playing the role of teacher. For some individuals, a life narrative interview provides a rare opportunity to enact this role.

While transmissive reminiscing is worthwhile, it should not be the main focus of the interview. The patient can end up being too focused on the narrow task of providing instruction, which eventually feels too much like a lecture for the listener.

Category 5, *negative reminiscence,* should definitely be avoided in the context of a life narrative interview. This type of reminiscing is driven by anxiety and has a predictable negative effect on the listener. *Obsessive reminiscence* is a common subtype that involves preoccupation with a few past events. The person repeats the same story over and over and is psychologically unable to resolve the negative feelings that it evokes. *Escapist reminiscence* is another subtype (Watt & Wong, 1991). Health care providers who work in Veterans Administration hospitals are familiar with elderly patients who recount in a hollow and repetitive manner their military experiences during World War II; these patients have no positive feelings about their current identity.

Fortunately, negative reminiscing represents only a small fraction of all reminiscing and is most often observed in individuals with cognitive impairments (e.g., poor short-term memory). When a patient is stuck in this mode, it is a difficult and trying experience for the interviewer and not likely to be as therapeutic for the patient.

REMINISCENCE THERAPY:
COUNSELING APPROACHES BASED ON REMINISCENCE

The idea of using reminiscence interviews as an intervention to enhance coping grew out of the numerous reminiscence therapy approaches that have been developed since the 1970s. These therapies were designed specifically to address the most common psychological problems of older adults (e.g., mild depression, low self-esteem, diminished life satisfaction). In 1963, Butler was the first to suggest that a therapist can facilitate and enhance an already ongoing process of life review. During the three decades since then, life review and other reminiscence techniques have become the most researched and most written-about intervention approaches in gerontology. A wide range of health professionals providing direct service to older adults—nurses, psychologists, social workers, recreation therapists, chaplains, and others—became enthusiastic practitioners and promoters of reminiscence therapies.

Research has generally supported the notion that reminiscence interventions have beneficial effects. For example, Haight (1988) found that 6 to 8 weeks of individual life review sessions with older people living in the community resulted in increased self-esteem and life satisfaction compared with a control group that received nonspecific social support. A study of a reminiscence therapy group for nursing home residents with some physical and cognitive impairments found reduced depression, compared with no change in a control group receiving supportive therapy (Goldwasser, Auerbach, & Harkins, 1987). Several other studies of group therapy found positive changes in attitude and mood measures (Ingersoll & Silverman, 1978; Reedy & Birren, 1980).

However, a careful review of the research findings suggests that reminiscence interventions alone are not sufficient treatment for serious mental health problems, such as depression (Thornton & Brotchie, 1987). For example, in one study of older adults with major depressive disorder, those in one group were treated with 12 sessions of reminiscence therapy and those in another group with 12 sessions of "social problem-solving" therapy. Reminiscence therapy was successful with only 30% of the subjects—as compared with 89% for social problem-solving therapy (Arean et al., 1993). By themselves, standard reminiscence or life review techniques may serve best as an approach to improving the life satisfaction and adjustment of "worried but well" elderly people. To provide effective treatment for serious mental health problems, reminiscence approaches probably need to be combined with other psychotherapy approaches, such as cognitive psychotherapy (see Watt & Cappeliez, 1995, for a description of one integrated technique).

More recently, modified reminiscence treatment approaches are being applied to a wide variety of populations (Haight & Hendrix, 1995). They have been used with hospice patients (Wholihan, 1991), Holocaust survivors (Schindler, 1992), elderly gays and lesbians (Galassie, 1991), female substance abusers (Woodhouse, 1992), and multigenerational families undergoing family therapy (DeGenova, 1991). One practitioner has written about a combined reminiscence and narrative counseling approach with younger adults facing catastrophic illness (Borden, 1992).

Although many articles have been written about outcomes of reminiscence therapy, there is surprisingly little specific "how to" information for conducting these interventions. The general descriptions that do appear in the literature, however, reveal some essential differences in reminiscence treatment approaches. For example, some group therapies focus on generational reminiscences (e.g., public events like presidential elections) while others focus on taking turns sharing personal reminiscences (e.g., comparing notes on early family experiences). Another difference is whether the counselor or group leader uses an *interpretive* approach or a *facilitative* approach.

With the *interpretive approach,* the counselor plays a more active role in trying to help the client integrate memories into a cohesive and positive life story. The most common interpretive approach is life review therapy (Lewis & Butler, 1974), which focuses on uncovering memories for which the client has unresolved feelings. The interpretive approaches to reminiscence therapy definitely require a trained, skilled counselor or therapist.

With the *facilitative approach,* on the other hand, the counselor takes on a primarily supportive role, approaching the older adult as a "wise teacher" (Burnside, 1978) and focusing mainly on rose-colored memories. As such, this approach requires little or no professional counseling training. The life narrative interviews presented in this book fit primarily into the facilitative category, although the "life challenges" interview in Chapter 7 may occasionally lead to interpretations by the interviewer.

NARRATIVE THERAPY: PSYCHOTHERAPY TECHNIQUES BASED ON PERSONAL NARRATIVES

A very recent trend toward using a narrative—storytelling—approach in psychotherapy influenced the development of the stress interventions discussed in this book. Though diverse in their methodology, these new narrative or storytelling approaches to the treatment of mental health problems are united by a set of basic assumptions: that development of identity involves the construction of a life story; that psychopathology is caused by life stories gone awry; and that psychotherapy is primarily an exercise in "repairing stories" (Howard, 1991). Narrative techniques are increasingly being used for patients with depression, eating disorders, psychosomatic disorders, chronic pain, and other mental health problems. One writer has heralded this growing movement as a "third wave" in psychotherapy (O'Hanlon, 1994).

The foundation for the narrative school of therapy was partly laid in the 1980s by a diverse group of theorists (Bruner, 1986; Polkinghorne, 1988; Sarbin, 1986). In essence, they all espoused the theory that putting events into a narrative story is the primary means by which our subjective experiences are made understandable and meaningful. A recent article aptly summarized this perspective: "The buzz of sensory experience would overwhelm us without some frame of reference. . . . So we collapse our experience into narrative structures, or stories, to make it more intelligible" (Cowley & Springen, 1995, p. 70). These stories, by necessity, emphasize some parts of our experience and leave others out.

At the same time, a group of developmental psychologists posited that all individuals base their identity on an ever-changing life story, or *personal narrative* (Cohler, 1982; Gergen & Gergen, 1983; McAdams, 1985). Cohler defined the personal narrative as "the most internally consistent interpretation of presently understood past, experienced present, and anticipated future" (p. 207). In formulating and reformulating our personal narrative, we strive to achieve a story that sounds internally consistent to us and others with whom we may share our stories. (This is similar to the previously mentioned concept of integrative reminiscence.) To meet this criterion, we necessarily put our own "spin" on events, and we give more weight to some life experiences and less to others.

This selectivity in choosing what to emphasize is precisely the point at which narrative therapists attempt to intervene. In his chapter entitled "Restorying a Life," Randall writes: ". . . we can regenerate our lives overall, in the same way as, over time, we frequently reframe individual events within them: today's horror on the highway becomes tomorrow's tragedy, next week's exciting adventure, next month's amusing anecdote, and old age's illustration of the irony of life" (p. 235)

Narrative approaches have much in common with the reminiscence approaches developed by professionals working with older adults. They both emphasize life stories told by patients and view the therapist more as a participant-guide than as an expert. Both approaches attempt to elicit positive stories about the self. As O'Hanlon put it, narrative therapists try to find positive stories from the patient's past to use as "a gateway to a parallel universe, one in which he or she is competent and heroic" (1994, p. 26).

However, narrative treatment approaches differ from reminiscence techniques in several important ways. First, narrative approaches are generally used by psychotherapists and family therapists who treat the mental health problems of individuals of all age groups. By contrast, reminiscence approaches are used primarily by allied health professionals working with older adults, as part of the overall care they provide. Second, reminiscence therapists try to work within an existing life story, to help the client get new perspectives on current issues or to facilitate the integration of unresolved past events and choices. In contrast, narrative therapists focus on changing, or "rewriting," dysfunctional stories about the self. They serve as cointerpreters, coaching the patient to make major revisions, changing the theme of the story from misfortune or tragedy into survival and triumph over adversity. Third, since they tend to deal with specific psychological disorders, narrative therapists usually focus on parts of the life story that deal with those aspects of the self, including stories about the present and future. In contrast, reminiscence counselors generally try to address all positive aspects of the individual's life story, focusing on the past exclusively.

Finally, unlike reminiscence counselors, narrative therapists include other types of treatment in their attempts to rewrite the patient's story, drawing heavily from family therapy and solution-oriented therapies. For example, one group of narrative therapists places a major emphasis on externalizing the client's problem (i.e., getting the patients to believe that "they are not the problem; the problem is the problem"; O'Hanlon, 1994, p. 24).

In summary, the interview techniques introduced in this book are based in part on the reminiscence theory and research covered in this chapter. The interviews we describe also incorporate some of the principles applied by reminiscence counselors and narrative therapists. However, our interviews differ from both approaches in that they are designed to be brief interventions aimed at augmenting the natural coping of patients who are facing stressful medical situations. They serve as a crisis intervention tool for typical patients, not as a method of psychotherapy or counseling to assist patients with clinical anxiety or depression.

REFERENCES

Arean, P. A., Perri, M. G., Nezu, A. M., Shein, R. L., Christopher, F., & Joseph, T. X. (1993). Comparative effectiveness of social problem-solving therapy and reminiscence therapy as treatments for depression in older adults. *Journal of Consulting and Clinical Psychology, 61* (6), 1003–1010.

Bandura, A. (1986). Self-efficacy mechanism in physiological activation and health-promoting behavior. In J. Madden, IV, S. Matthysse, & J. Barchas (Eds.), *Adaptation, learning and affect* (pp. 1–51). New York: Raven.

Borden, W. (1992). Narrative perspectives in psychosocial intervention following adverse life events. *Social Work, 37,* 135–141.

Brink, T. L. (1979). *Geriatric psychotherapy.* New York: Human Sciences.

Bruner, J. S. (1986). *Actual minds, possible worlds.* Cambridge, MA: Harvard University Press.

Burnside, I. M. (1978). In I. M. Burnside (Ed.), *Working with the elderly: Group processes and techniques.* New York: Duxbury Press.

Butler, R. N. (1963). The life review: An interpretation of reminiscence in the aged. *Psychiatry, 26,* 65–76.

Casey, E. S. (1989). *Remembering: A phenomenological study.* Bloomington, IN: Indiana University Press.

Cohler, B. (1982). Personal narrative and life course. In P. Baltes & O. Brim (Eds.), *Life-span development and behavior* (Vol. 4, pp. 205–241). San Diego, CA: Academic.

Coleman, P. G. (1974). Measuring reminiscence characteristics from conversation as adaptive features of old age. *Journal of Aging and Human Development, 5,* 281–294.

Cowley, G., & Springen, K. (1995, April 17). Rewriting life stories. *Newsweek,* 70–74.

DeGenova, M. (1991). Elderly life review therapy: A Bowen approach. *American Journal of Family Therapy, 19,* 160–166.

Erikson, E. (1950). *Childhood and society.* New York: Norton.

Fallot, R. (1980). The impact on mood of verbal reminiscing in later adulthood. *International Journal of Aging and Human Development, 10,* 385–400.

Galassie, F. (1991). A life-review workshop for gay and lesbian elders. *Journal of Gerontological Social Work, 16,* 75–86.

Gergen, K., & Gergen, M. (1983). Narratives of the self. In T. R. Sarbin & K. E. Scheibe (Eds.), *Studies in social identity* (pp. 254–273). New York: Praeger.

Goldwasser, N., Auerbach, S. M., & Harkins, S. (1987). Cognitive, affective and behavioral effects of reminiscence group therapy with demented elderly. *International Journal of Aging and Human Development, 25,* 209–222.

Gutmann, D. (1990). *Reclaimed Powers: Toward a new psychology of men and women in later life.* New York: Basic.

Haight, B. K. (1988). The therapeutic role of structured life review process in homebound elderly subjects. *Journal of Gerontology, 43,* 40–44.

Haight, B. K., & Hendrix, S. (1995). An integrated review of reminiscence. In B. K. Haight & J. D. Webster (Eds.). *The art and science of reminiscing: Theory, research, methods, and applications* (pp. 3–21). Washington, DC: Taylor & Francis.

Havinghurst, R. J., & Glasser, R. (1972). An exploratory study of reminiscence. *Journal of Gerontology, 27,* 245–253.
Howard, G. S. (1991). A narrative approach to thinking, cross-cultural psychology, and psychotherapy. *American Psychologist, 46,* 187–197.
Hyland, D. T., & Ackerman, A. M. (1988). Reminiscence and autobiographical memory in the study of the personal past. *Journal of Gerontology, 43,* 35–39.
Ingersoll, B., & Silverman, A. (1978). Comparative group psychotherapy for the aged. *The Gerontologist, 18,* 201–206.
Kaufman, S. R. (1986). *The Ageless Self: Sources of meaning in late life.* Madison, WI: University of Wisconsin Press.
Lewis, C. N. (1971). Reminiscing and self-concept in old age. *Journal of Gerontology, 26,* 240–243.
Lewis, M. I., & Butler, R. N. (1974). Life review therapy. *Geriatrics, 29,* 165–173.
LoGerfo, M. (1980). Three ways of reminiscence in theory and practice. *International Journal of Aging and Human Development, 12,* 39–49.
McAdams, D. P. (1985). *Power, intimacy, and the life story: Personological inquiries into identity.* Homewood, IL: Dorsey.
Merriam, S. B., & Cross, L. (1982). Adulthood and reminiscence: A descriptive study. *Educational Gerontology, 8,* 275–290.
O'Hanlon, B. (1994, November-December). The third wave. *Networker,* 18–29.
Polkinghorne, D. E. (1988). *Narrative knowing and the human sciences.* Albany: State University of New York Press.
Priefer, B. A., & Gambert, S. R. (1984). Reminiscence and life review in the elderly. *Psychiatric Medicine, 2,* 91–100.
Randall, W. L. (1996). Restorying a life: Adult education and transformative learning. In J. E. Birren, G. M. Keynon, J. E. Ruth, J. J. F. Schroots, T. Svensson (Eds.) *Aging and biography: Explorations in adult development.* New York Springer.
Reedy, M. N., & Birren, J. E. (1980). *Life review through guided autobiography.* Paper presented at the annual meeting of the American Psychological Association, Montreal, Quebec, Canada.
Romaniuk, M., & Romaniuk, J. G. (1981). Looking back: An analysis of reminiscence functions and triggers. *Experimental Aging Research, 7,* 477–489.
Romaniuk, M., & Romaniuk, J. G. (1983). Life events and reminiscence: A comparison of the memories of young and old adults. *Imagination, Cognition, and Personality, 2,* 125–136.
Sarbin, T. R. (Ed.). (1986). *Narrative psychology: The storied nature of human conduct.* New York: Praeger.
Schindler, R. (1992). Silences: Helping elderly holocaust victims deal with the past. *International Journal of Aging and Human Development, 35,* 243–252.
Sherman, E. (1991). *Reminiscence and the self in old age.* New York: Springer.
Thornton, S., & Brotchie, J. (1987). Reminiscence: A critical review of the empirical literature. *British Journal of Clinical Psychology, 26,* 93–111.
Watt, L., & Cappeliez, P. (1995). Reminiscence interventions for the treatment of depression in older adults. In B. K. Haight & J. D. Webster (Eds.), *The art and science of reminiscing: Theory, research, methods, and applications* (pp. 221–232). Washington, DC: Taylor & Francis.
Webster, J. D. (1994). Predictors of reminiscence: A lifespan perspective. *Canadian Journal on Aging, 13,* 66–78.

Webster, J. D. (1995). Adult age differences in reminiscence functions. In B. K. Haight & J. D. Webster (Eds.), *The art and science of reminiscing: Theory, research, methods, and applications* (pp. 221–232). Washington, DC: Taylor & Francis.

Wholihan, D. (1991). The value of reminiscence in hospice care. *American Journal of Hospice and Palliative Care, 9,* 33–35.

Wong, P. T. P. (1995). The processes of adaptive reminiscences. In B. K. Haight & J. D. Webster (Eds.), *The art and science of reminiscing: Theory, research, methods, and applications* (pp. 23–36). Washington, DC: Taylor & Francis.

Wong, P. T. P., & Watt, L. M. (1991). What types of reminiscence are associated with successful aging? *Psychology and Aging, 6,* 272–279.

Woodhouse, L. (1992). Women with jagged edges: Voices from a culture of substance abuse. *Qualitative Health Research, 2,* 262–281.

CHAPTER 3

Developing and Testing
Two Types of
Life Narrative Interviews*

---

*The past sharpens perspective, warns of pitfalls,
and helps point the way.—Dwight D. Eisenhower*

This chapter will describe the two types of life narrative interviews we have developed for stress intervention in a medical setting. It will also review the two studies that were conducted to assess the efficacy of these two interviews. We conclude with a summary of the research findings and their implications for health care professionals who may want to use life narrative techniques.

OVERVIEW: TWO LIFE NARRATIVE INTERVIEWS

For the past 10 years, my colleagues and I (B. Rybarczyk) have worked on developing and testing 1-hour life narrative interviews to serve as stress interventions for medical patients (Rybarczyk, 1988; Rybarczyk, 1995; Rybarczyk & Auerbach, 1990; Rybarczyk, Auerbach, Jorn, Lofland, & Perlman, 1993). Our initial exploration of the reminiscence literature

*A large portion of this chapter was taken from Rybarczyk, 1995, and is used with permission of Taylor & Francis.

27

led to two approaches to enhancing coping: (1) the *life experience interview* elicits the patient's life story primarily in the form of simple reminiscence; (2) the *life challenges interview* has the additional goal of encouraging mastery reminiscence. Our intention was to test both interviews to determine which was a more effective stress intervention. However, two studies (described in the next sections) indicated that both interviews are efficacious, each having unique advantages—though each of them also has some disadvantages.

The two interviews have the same basic goals. Both employ the interviewer as a participant-listener who directs the patient's telling of the life story, or life narrative, through chronologically ordered anecdotes. The focus is on positive events only. Both interviews also use a semistructured format, striking a balance between asking questions to provide direction and allowing the participant to free-associate spontaneously from topic to topic. To steer the patient toward positive areas, the interviewer needs specific skills and a set of topics. In both interviews, the interviewer implicitly conveys that the goal is not to gather information but to create a positive psychological experience for the storyteller.

The *life experience interview* (LEI) is the simpler of the two interviews. This approach is based on the premise that the positive feelings elicited by simple reminiscing will effectively counteract anxiety triggered by a stressful situation. The LEI covers topics that frequently evoke positive emotions, such as childhood activities, family traditions, adventures in adolescence, and early dating experiences. No direct effort is made to guide the interviewee toward remembering events that relate to successful coping.

The more advanced *life challenges interview* (LCI) builds on the goals of the LEI, with additional emphasis on mastery reminiscence. Although the LCI, like the LEI, invites interviewees to tell their life stories, it differs significantly from the LEI in that the interviewer does guide patients toward stories about challenges successfully met (e.g., surviving the great depression, doing well in school, getting a first job). The overall goal of the LCI is to increase interviewees' awareness of their coping strengths and resources by directing them to recall past successes in meeting life's challenges. On the emotional level, the goal of the LCI is to decrease anxiety and increase participants' sense of satisfaction, pride, and accomplishment. On the cognitive level, the goal is to heighten the participants' awareness of positive strengths and resources they have used to meet challenges. Patients' increased awareness of their coping resources presumably minimizes the perception that the medical stress they are facing is overwhelming.

Although we believe that life narrative interviews are appropriate for people of all ages, our research originally focused on people age 50 and older. Three factors encouraged us to target older adults for this intervention. First, the current cohort of older adults tend to be reluctant to participate in the standard mental health interventions that are offered to medical patients (e.g., counseling, relaxation training). Second, older adults have a wealth of life experiences to draw on. Third, people over 50 constitute the vast majority of acute care hospital admissions, undergo the largest number of invasive procedures, and stay in the hospital for the longest periods of time (American College of Surgeons, 1987).

INITIAL STUDY: RICHMOND, VIRGINIA*

In 1987, we conducted the first stress intervention study using the two life narrative interviews, the LEI and the LCI. This study was done at the McGuire Veterans Administration Hospital in Richmond, Virginia (Rybarczyk, 1988; Rybarczyk & Auerbach, 1990). The 104 veterans who participated (mean age = 65.7 years) were facing a variety of elective surgical procedures: the most common ones were coronary bypass, prostate resection, and hernia repair. Interviews were conducted the afternoon or evening before surgery and lasted between 45 minutes and 1 hour. Interviewers were males who were either graduate students in psychology (age range = 24–31 years) or older adults recruited from other volunteer programs (age range = 63–72 years). Interviewers received 1 hour of individual training, were given a written set of suggested topics to cover, and were given feedback after each interview audiotape had been reviewed by the first author.

Four groups were compared. One group received an LEI; a second group received an LCI; a third group received a "placebo" (or "attention only") interview that focused on present interests and activities; and a control group received no intervention. In addition, the effectiveness of the psychology graduate students and the older adult volunteers was compared. Because the interviews were not complicated and capitalized on what is considered to be a skill that improves over the life span, we hypothesized that the older adult peer counselors would be as effective as the psychology graduate students.

We had expected that only about half of the older male veterans who were invited to participate in a psychological intervention would agree

---

*Readers who may be less interested in detailed descriptions of the research studies supporting this work may want to skip to the end of this chapter for a summary of the most important findings.

to do so, but 85% of those invited agreed to be in the study. This supports the notion that reminiscence is inherently appealing as a basis for psychological intervention. By and large, participants seemed to view it as an honor that someone was taking an interest in their life story. The original plan was to audiotape the interview solely as a means of monitoring what was happening during the interview, so that feedback could be provided to the interviewers. In retrospect, judging by the comments of the participants, the presence of the recorder seemed to give a sense of importance to the interview.

Overall, the results were very encouraging. Subjects who participated in either of the two reminiscence interviews experienced a decrease in anxiety after the interview, compared with an increase in anxiety among the subjects who received the present-focus interview or no interview (see Figure 3.1). An anxiety pretest was given several hours before the interview and a posttest within 1 hour afterward. A four-item version of the State-Trait Anxiety Inventory (STAI) (Spielberger, Gorsuch, & Lushene, 1970) was used both times. The present-focus group and the control group were given the same pretest and posttest, separated by an interval equivalent to that in the other groups.

As hypothesized, in addition to a reduction in anxiety, both the LCI group and LEI group had higher scores on the Coping Self-Efficacy Inventory than the other two groups. This scale was used to directly measure the degree of confidence individuals have in their coping skills and resources (see Appendix A; three items were adapted from a scale by Tipton & Worthington, 1984). The results also showed that the greatest increase in coping self-efficacy occurred in patients who had been interviewed by older volunteers. Thus the LCI did have the largest positive effect on the patients' awareness of their coping strengths and resources, but only when it was administered by age-peers (see Figure 3.2). Similarly, the LCI interviews conducted by the older volunteers led to greater reductions on the STAI than those conducted by graduate students.

This finding agreed with previous research showing that volunteer peer counselors are as effective as professionals when administering structured interventions to people who are "worried but well" (Durlak, 1979). A review of the audiotapes suggested that the better performance of the older LCI interviewers was related to the fact that they had lived through the same time period and could relate to many events being discussed in the interview. A greater level of kinship, trust, and openness between members of the same generation also may have played a role.

The statistically significant differences obtained in any study of a psychological intervention need to be evaluated further to determine if they

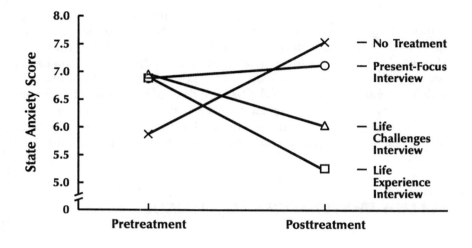

FIGURE 3.1   Study 1: Pre- and posttreatment state anxiety scores.

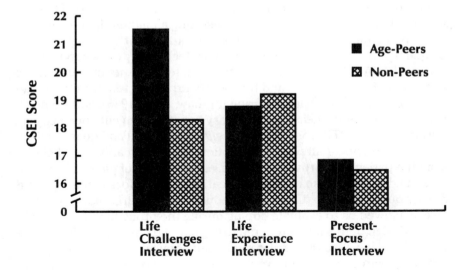

FIGURE 3.2   Study 1: Posttreatment scores on the Coping Self-Efficacy
Inventory (CSEI).

are clinically significant (Ludwick-Rosenthal & Neufeld, 1988). One approach to evaluating whether individual patients experienced a tangible benefit from the intervention is to examine the size of the effect (Cohen, 1977). Using a formula suggested by Hedges and Olkin (1985), we obtained effect sizes 1.8 and 0.77 on the anxiety and coping self-efficacy measures, respectively. Using guidelines proposed by Cohen, these sizes can be characterized as "very strong." In addition, these effects were greater than those obtained in the majority of more than 30 studies of presurgical stress intervention reviewed by Suls and Wan (1989).

FOLLOW-UP STUDY: CHICAGO, ILLINOIS

To replicate and extend the findings from the first study, we undertook an 18-month study, funded by the American Association of Retired Persons' Andrus Foundation (Rybarczyk, Auerbach, Jorn, Lofland, & Perlman, 1993). This study was conducted at Rush-Presbyterian-St. Luke's Medical Center in Chicago and included 143 patients (mean age = 65 years; 96 males, 47 females). Rather than using a variety of surgical patients as in the initial study, we included only patients who were undergoing a specific balloon angioplasty procedure, PTCA. This is a very common procedure; it involves inserting a balloon-tipped catheter into one or more coronary arteries and inflating it to compress the plaque that obstructs blood flow. Although technically not a surgical procedure, PTCA is known to be very stressful for patients because of the substantial risk it involves and the fact that they are required to remain conscious and to participate during it (Shaw, et al., 1986). Our homogeneous sample let us measure secondary benefits from enhanced coping during and after PTCA. *Secondary benefits* are medical and quasi-medical benefits that appear after an intervention and presumably would derive from the patient's improved coping: e.g., perception of pain, nurses' ratings of adjustment, use of pain medication, days before discharge, and 30-day outcome. Also, using a procedure that required patients to be awake allowed us to evaluate coping during the procedure.

The design of this study differed from that of the initial study in three ways. First, because the earlier study had showed that they compared favorably with younger adult volunteers, we used older adult volunteers only. There were 19 volunteers (mean age = 66.2 years; 14 females, 5 males). Second, in lieu of a present-focus interview, a comparison group of patients received a combination of established relaxation training interventions (Aiken & Henrichs, 1971; Corah, Gale, Pace, & Seyrek, 1981), including diaphragmatic breathing, progressive muscle relaxation, and visualization. Third, the training time for volunteers was increased from 1 hour in the classroom to 4 hours, and a practice session with non-surgical patients was added.

On a qualitative level, the social characteristics of the subjects differed substantially from those in the first study. The previous subjects were men who had lived most of their lives in rural Virginia and West Virginia. In this second study, the subjects were both men and women, most of whom had been born and raised in a large midwestern city. A large sub-group of the Chicago residents had emigrated from central and eastern Europe during the 1930s and 1940s. This meant that the stories elicited during their LCIs shifted from the burdens of daily farm life or working in coal mines to urban life in Chicago's ethnic neighborhoods and life in the "old country." The inclusion of women and adults as young as 50 meant that a broader array of topics and questions had to be covered in the interviews. For instance, we found that women in their sixties who had careers often related rich stories about the challenges they faced as pioneers in the workplace.

As in the initial study, a range of findings supported the overall efficacy of this type of intervention. First, both life narrative interviews—the LEI and the LCI—led to a significant reduction in anxiety scores (in contrast to an increase in anxiety for the "no treatment" group), using the same instrument and measurement points as the first study. Second, the reductions in anxiety obtained as a result of storytelling were comparable to those obtained as a result of relaxation training (see Figure 3.3). Third, all three groups (as compared with the controls) reported using more emotion-focused coping, on an abbreviated Ways of Coping Checklist. Last, patients in all three intervention groups reported greater satisfaction than the controls with the preparation and scheduling of the PCTA procedure; thus they perceived the hospital as a whole as providing better services. In general, the effect sizes were only slightly smaller than those in the first study, ranging from "moderate" to "strong" according to Cohen's 1977 criteria.

As in the first study, a pair of findings confirmed the unique effect that the LCI has on the appraisal aspect of coping. The LCI group reported significantly more positive thinking than the controls on a validated measure of positive and negative self-statements (Kendall, Williams, Pechacek, Graham, Shisslak, & Herzoff, 1979). In addition, only the LCI subjects had significantly higher scores than controls on the coping self-efficacy measure. The other two intervention groups scored higher than the controls but less than the LCI subjects, but neither difference was

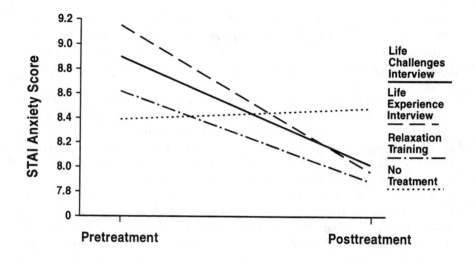

FIGURE 3.3   Study 2: Pre- and posttreatment state anxiety scores on the State-Trait Anxiety Inventory (STAI).

significant. Both of these findings support the hypothesis that a life narrative interview focused on challenging events stimulates an increase in patients' awareness of their coping abilities.

However, in contrast to the positive findings on measures of coping, the intervention had no demonstrable secondary benefits. In this study, there were no positive findings for nurses' rating of adjustment during the PTCA procedure, for perception of pain during the PTCA, for use of pain medication after the PTCA, for days between PTCA and discharge, or for quality of life and psychological adjustment 30 days after the procedure.

The lack of secondary medical benefits has several plausible explanations. First, it may be that coping interventions of this type enhance only psychological coping and do not cross over the mind-body barrier to provide medical benefits per se. Second, since the PTCA procedure is relatively routine and not very physically demanding, it may not have provided enough of an opportunity for such a crossover. Third, it is possible that benefits did exist but could not be detected with our crude measurements. Previous research on stress intervention has been mixed in terms of demonstrating a connection between patients' level of coping and various medical outcomes (Anderson & Masur, 1983). When any effects have been demonstrated, they have often been small and have required sophisticated assessment techniques (e.g., immunological tests, standardized observer rating scales) not used in this study. Future studies of life narrative intervention will attempt to demonstrate secondary benefits in patients undergoing more physically demanding procedures than the PTCA, with an eye toward improving the measurement of these benefits.

In the second study, as noted, we included women as well as men and patients who were as young as age 50. However, we found that a patient's gender, educational status, and age had no influence on the efficacy of the life narrative interventions. This lends support to the idea that the benefits of reminiscence cut across gender and age barriers. Borden (1992) has posited that similar life narrative interventions can play a key role in helping younger adult patients adjust to catastrophic medical illness. Although the literature of the past 20 years generally assumes that reminiscence is a critical element of psychological adjustment only in the latter portion of the life span, several studies suggest that age is not a factor in the frequency or function of reminiscence (Hyland & Ackerman, 1988; Merriam & Cross, 1982; Romaniuk & Romaniuk, 1983).

Finally, one very encouraging finding with regard to the efficacy of life narrative interviews was the exceptional results obtained by a subset of volunteers in both studies. For instance, in the second study, when the four most effective volunteers from the LEI and LCI groups (two in each) were examined separately, the 22 subjects they interviewed showed an average decrease of 2.2 points on the STAI. In contrast, the average decrease in anxiety for the remaining 49 subjects interviewed by the other 12 volunteers was 0.4. The variability among the volunteers who provided the relaxation training was negligible. Thus the results of life narrative interviews would probably be improved substantially by using more stringent criteria for selecting the interviewers and improving the training.

SUMMARY OF THE RESEARCH FINDINGS

Our two studies demonstrated that life narrative interviews are effective tools for enhancing the coping of medical patients. Two types of interviews—LEI and LCI—provided measurable benefits for the patient, the hospital, and even the volunteers. The following points summarize the important findings:

1. Life narrative interviews lead to substantial reductions in the anxiety that patients commonly experience when facing an invasive medical procedure.

2. Life narrative interviews are as effective as the relaxation techniques and interventions widely used in health care settings to alleviate stress.
3. When an interview focuses on past experiences of successful coping, it leads to a positive change in the patient's appraisal of his or her coping abilities and resources. Previous research has shown that these beliefs about self-efficacy play an important role in behavioral outcomes.
4. A 45-minute life narrative interview is far more effective at reducing stress than a social support session for an equivalent length of time.
5. Patients who have much on their minds and are facing a stressful medical procedure are nonetheless receptive to participating in a life narrative interview. Coping aside, almost all participants find the interview interesting and enjoyable.
6. Future studies of the benefits of life narrative interviews need to use more sophisticated and more accurate methods of measuring health benefits.
7. Properly trained volunteers are effective life narrative interviewers. In addition, they find interviewing to be a highly satisfying assignment.
8. There are no apparent age or gender limitations on the benefits of life narrative interviews. Both men and women and individuals from all the age groups studied benefited equally from participation in the interviews.

REFERENCES

Aiken, L. H., & Henrichs, T. F. (1971). Systematic relaxation as a nursing intervention technique with open heart surgery patients. *Nursing Research, 20,* 212–217.

American College of Surgeons (1987). *Socio-economic factbook for surgery 1987.* Chicago: Author.

Anderson, K. O., & Masur, F. T. (1983). Psychological preparation for invasive medical and dental procedures. *Journal of Behavioral Medicine, 6,* 1–40.

Borden, W. (1992). Narrative perspectives in psychosocial intervention following adverse life events. *Social Work, 37,* 135–141.

Cohen, J. (1977). *Statistical power analysis for the behavioral sciences.* San Diego, CA: Academic.

Corah, N. L., Gale, E. N., Pace, L. F., & Seyrek, S. K. (1981). Relaxation and muscle programming as a means of reducing psychological stress during dental procedures. *Journal of the American Dental Association, 103,* 232–234.

Durlak, J. A. (1979). Comparative effectiveness of paraprofessionals and professional helpers. *Psychological Bulletin, 86,* 80–92.

Hedges, L. V., & Olkin, I. (1985). *Statistical methods for meta-analysis.* San Diego, CA: Academic.

Hyland, D. T., & Ackerman, A. M. (1988). Reminiscence and autobiographical memory in the study of the personal past. *Journal of Gerontology, 43,* 35–39.

Kendall, P. C., Williams, L., Pechacek, T. F., Graham, L. E., Shisslak, C., & Herzoff, N. (1979). Cognitive-behavioral and patient education interventions in cardiac catheterization procedures: The Palo Alto medical psychology project. *Journal of Consulting and Clinical Psychology, 47,* 49–58.

Ludwick-Rosenthal, R., & Neufeld, R. W. J. (1988). Stress management during noxious medical procedures: An evaluative review of outcome studies. *Psychological Bulletin, 104,* 326–342.

Merriam, S. B., & Cross, L. (1982). Adulthood and reminiscence: A descriptive study. *Educational Gerontology, 8,* 275–290.

Romaniuk, M., & Romaniuk, J. G. (1983). Life events and reminiscence: A comparison of the memories of young and old adults. *Imagination, Cognition, and Personality, 2,* 125–136.

Rybarczyk, B. D. (1988). Two types of reminiscence interviews for coping enhancement: A presurgical intervention tailored for older adults. *Dissertation Abstracts International, 49,* 4021B. (University Microfilms No. 88-26, 976)

Rybarcsyk, B. (1995). Using reminiscence interviews for stress management in the medical setting. In B. K. Haight & J. Webster (Eds.) *The art and science of reminiscing: Theory, research, methods, and applciations* (pp. 205–217). Washinton, DC: Taylor & Francis.

Rybarczyk, B. D. & Auerbach, S. M. (1990). Reminiscence interviews as stress management interventions for older patients undergoing surgery. *The Gerontologist, 30,* 522–528.

Rybarczyk, B. D., Auerbach, S. M., Jorn, M., Lofland, K., & Perlman, M. (1993). Using volunteers and reminiscence to help older adults cope with an invasive medical procedure: A follow-up study. *Behavior, Health, and Aging, 3,* 147–162.

Shaw, R. E., Cohen, F., Fishman-Rosen, J., Murphy, M. C., Stertzer, S. H., Clark, D. A., & Myler, R. K. (1986). Psychological predictors of psychosocial and medical outcomes in patients undergoing coronary angioplasty. *Psychosomatic Medicine, 48,* 582–597.

Spielberger, C. D., Gorsuch, R., & Lushene, R. L. (1970). *Manual for the state anxiety inventory.* Palo Alto, CA: Consulting Psychologist Press.

Suls, J., & Wan, C. K. (1989). Effects of sensory and procedural information on coping with stressful medical procedures and pain: A meta-analysis. *Journal of Consulting and Clinical Psychology, 57,* 372–379.

Tipton, R. M. & Worthington, E. L. (1984). The measurement of generalized self-efficacy: A study of construct validity. *Journal of Personality Assessment., 48,* 545–549.

CHAPTER 4

Nine Process Goals for Life Narrative Interviews

Every person's life is worth a novel. —E. Polster (1977)

The goal of life narrative interviewing is not to gather information but to create a positive psychological experience for the storyteller. To put this more succinctly, "The process is more important than the product" (American Association of Retired Persons [AARP], 1989). This is in contrast to most interviews, which attempt to obtain certain critical information (e.g., a medical history or the qualifications of a job applicant).

Two key issues determine the quality of a life narrative interview. First, the interviewer needs to create an atmosphere that encourages patients to express their life stories in a lively, free-flowing, creative manner. Methods for accomplishing this are emphasized throughout this chapter. Second, there needs to be a positive interaction between the storyteller and storylistener; this factor will be covered in the chapter on effective listening (Chapter 6).

As a result of supervising and completing hundreds of interviews, we have formulated nine basic *process goals* that serve as guidelines (see Table 4.1). We call them process goals because they focus on the storytelling process and the listening process, not on specific content or the desired outcome of the interview. When interviewers focus on achieving the process goals, moment by moment, what they would like to happen in the interview as a whole will naturally follow.

39

TABLE 4.1   Nine Process Goals

1. Balance guidance with spontaneity.
2. Show, don't tell.
3. Celebrate the positive.
4. Make it personal.
5. Follow the threads chronologically.
6. Get the big picture.
7. Keep it fresh.
8. Encourage reflection.
9. Be prepared.

GOAL 1:
BALANCE GUIDANCE WITH SPONTANEITY

Life narrative interviews are usually best when the interviewer uses a semistructured format. Ideally, a balance is struck between "I ask the questions, you give the answers" and allowing the storyteller to free-associate spontaneously from topic to topic. The situation is similar to ballroom dancing, in that too much control makes the result stiff and uninteresting but too little guidance results in chaos. Therefore, the interviewer leads the storyteller to ensure that the goals of the interview are accomplished, but spontaneity must be encouraged from the outset.

The life narrative interview will be a new unique situation for the interviewee, so he or she will be looking for hints as to what is expected. For instance, the interviewer should be cautious about reeling off a series of questions, either memorized or on paper, since the storyteller may assume that brief answers should be given to satisfy the interviewer's request for information. As one physician put it, "If you ask questions, you will get answers, and nothing else" (Balint, 1964). Instead, the patient should be given the message that the interview is a collaborative venture. The role of the interviewer is to ask questions and make facilitative comments that lead the storyteller into lively stories about topics that both find interesting.

The following interview with a 58-year-old man undergoing chemotherapy for colon cancer illustrates a good balance of guidance and spontaneity. The interviewer (I) begins this segment with a creative question and then steps back, using facilitative comments and questions only. At one point, the patient (P) begins to drift into a description of his hobby, but the interviewer is successful in steering him back to storytelling.

I: *What kinds of things did you do with your kids when they were growing up?*
P: I taught them to be rock hounds.
I: *What is that?*
P: Well, rock-hounding is when you look for rocks that are different, particularly fossils.
I: *Oh, that kind of rock hounding. Fossil hunting. Okay.*
P: Yeah, that kind. We actually made several different trips. One to Wyoming. One to California. Rock-hounding all the way.
I: *Those are major expeditions.*
P: We just had a great time as a family. We would even slab and polish stones together. In Elmhurst there's a museum called the Lizzadro Museum. And they teach courses on cabochon cutting and polishing. Cabochon is rock also. And so it's a wonderful museum. If you ever have a chance to go there, go through that museum.
I: *[Interrupts.] I would like to. I love fossils and rocks. Tell me about those trips that you took. They sound like real adventures.*
P: We had some interesting experiences. I remember one of the places that we kind of used as our headquarters for one trip was Rock Springs, Wyoming.
I: *I've heard of Rock Springs.*
P: Right on I-80. There is a huge—I don't know if its still there—retail rock shop. I was looking around there one day and I said, "Where in the world did you get these algae and tortilla rocks?" And he said, "I'll draw you a little map." So he drew us a little map, and it was down past this town called Rawlings. And he said, "You turn here to the right, go past the gate, you'll see a shepherd's house, and then you turn right and you drive up to this plateau. You'll find all kinds of algae and tortilla rocks." Tortilla rock is a black rock full of snails.
I: *Okay.*
P: But he says, "If it starts to rain up there, you get out, because that red soil becomes slick as glass." And darn it, if it didn't start to rain as soon as we got there.
I: *Oh, no!*
P: When we got up there—well, you had to come down off of that plateau on a very steep winding road.
I: *And it was all that red clay that he told you about.*
P: You bet.
I: *Oh, dear.*
P: And my wife had two fits. She just couldn't believe that we were ever going to get out of that mess! But we did. [With satisfaction.]
I: *Was it a dangerous ride down?*
P: Oh, yes! Oh, sure! You'd hit the brakes and try to hold the brakes but you'd just slip and slide.

I: *How did the kids handle it?*

P: They thought it was great. [Both laugh.] Another situation happened when we went looking for jade and we didn't know where to look. So we asked this fellow, and he said, "Well, you can find it up in here."

I: *You're still in Wyoming?*

P: Yes, in Wyoming. So we got up there and looked around. And we found one piece of jade and one arrowhead. And it was getting kind of late, and at just some remote crossroads there was a diner-type restaurant. So we stopped in there to eat. It was just my family and a husband and a wife sitting across the way. And when they got up to leave, they both had six-guns. So as they passed us, I said, "Why do you carry your six-guns out here?" And they said, "Well, when you go out and look for jade, there are rattlesnakes, and we shoot the rattlesnakes." [Laughing.] Here we looked for jade all day long!

I: *[Interviewer laughs with patient.]*

P: And my wife almost died.

I: *Well, it sounds like she had some traumatic times on these trips.*

P: That's right.

GOAL 2: SHOW, DON'T TELL

It is far more effective for the patient to focus on vivid, rich sensory images than to merely relate factual information—who, what, where. The sensory aspects of a story are the most interesting and personally engaging for both storyteller and listener. When speakers describe events in dry, general terms, we yearn for them to give us a "sense" or "flavor" of what it was like to be there. This is what writers of fiction and creative nonfiction do all the time, because this is the type of writing that is most interesting to readers. The interviewer's task in life narrative interviewing is to help the storyteller create a "best-seller" as opposed to a dull historical account.

To do this, the interviewer often may need to express interest in a particular topic glossed over by the storyteller and ask to hear more vivid, more descriptive sensory details related to what the storyteller saw, heard, smelled, tasted, or felt. If the storyteller offers an overview without many images or skips rapidly from topic to topic, the interviewer can try to slow down the interview by suggesting that they go over a particular area again in detail. Paradoxically, this suggestion—"Slow down"— is particularly important when there are time constraints on the interview. In such cases, focusing on describing just a few images can be more effective than being comprehensive (goal 6).

Sometimes the opposite happens, however: the patient is ready to tell a richly detailed story, but the interviewer gets in the way. This was the case in an interview with a 63-year-old woman who was hospitalized for extensive tests. The interviewer (I) asked some closed-ended questions that slowed things down, but even so the patient (P) was able to get into the spirit of storytelling.

P: We had next-door neighbors, Mr. and Mrs. Reynolds and I used to take care of their little son, Bobby. I'd walk him up and down the sidewalk in the buggy.

I: *How old were you then?*

P: I was about 8 or 9.

I: *So you were still very young.*

P: Yeah. But I would still walk him up and down. She would put him in the buggy, and I would walk him up and down the sidewalk. About a five-house radius, you know.

I: *Sure.*

P: Our houses were so close together, and she and my mother were good friends. She'd holler out the one bedroom window and into our bedroom window. My mother would put the ironing board out there across the two windowsills, and then she'd push something over with a stick, like a pie or a fresh loaf of bread, something like that.

I: *Oh, how clever!*

P: And they'd push things back and forth like that.

I: *It was a real neighborhood back in those days.*

After a time, the patient had developed rapport with the interviewer, and to keep the ball rolling the interviewer simply had to remain interested.

I: *What did your mother do?*

P: She cleaned houses, and she worked for a lady that had five or six kids. They had a little dog they called Spot. It was born without a tail. And the woman told my mother that she wanted to give the dog to somebody because she was afraid her kids were going to hurt him; they were rough. So my mother brought Spot home to me, and I remember the kids coming along, and they were crying and I was crying with them. I said, "I'll take good care of him." I said, "I'll love him a whole lot." [Laughs at memory.]

I: *[Interviewer laughs along with patient.]*

P: They were so sad to lose their puppy. Of course, I babied it something terrible. I remember in the basement there was a long hall, it was linoleum, and my mother kept it waxed. She'd have rag rugs, you know. Spot found out that if he started in the front room and really gathered up steam and sat down on the rug, he'd slide all the way to the back door. [Laughs.]

I: *Smart dog! [Laughs with patient.]*

P: My mother couldn't figure out why that rug was always laying by the back door all crumpled up. And one day she saw what he was doing. He was taking a ride on the rug!

The most vivid sensory images are not necessarily visual; it's often useful to ask about sounds, smells, and tastes. Here's an example from a 72-year-old man who was awaiting surgery on the day of the interview. (I = interviewer; P = patient.)

I: *Do you remember any Christmas or Easter treats? Like hot cross buns?*
P: Oh—my mother used to bake coffee cakes from yeast. Risen yeast.
I: *Wow.*
P: Where it would be rising all night long, and then we'd have fresh-baked coffee cake with butter and sugar and cinnamon on it.
I: *Oh, yes—and you could smell it baking.*
P: Yes. Very aromatic. It was the greatest thing to have fresh, yeast-risen bread.

GOAL 3: CELEBRATE THE POSITIVE

There are rich veins of gold in a patient's memories that directly facilitate reducing stress, strengthening the patient's sense of positive identity, and underscoring personal strengths and resources. The positive focus of the life narrative interview is designed to elicit such memories, some of which might not have been accessible to the patient for years. Beneficial emotional effects are plainly evident in the following exchange with a 76-year-old woman whose parents had emigrated from Poland. (P = patient; I = interviewer.)

P: You see, everybody came to my mother.
I: *Oh, really?*
P: Whoever came from the "old country," they came straight to my mother. Until they found a place of their own. Because my mother always fixed the attic with beds—a place for all the newcomers to stay.
I: *That's marvelous. Can you remember those people staying upstairs?*
P: Oh, lots of them. There were some real characters. [Laughing.] They used to dance in the kitchen. With my mother. We had one of those old Victrolas, you know. [Moves her hands in a cranking motion.] All the furniture and everything got moved. And they'd dance.
I: *Sounds like fun.*
P: My father was a little jealous.
I: *Oh, he was?*

P: Sure. Everybody would like to dance with my mother. They would polka across the room and turn around at the wall. [Both laugh.] They would have so much fun. We should have had cameras back then.

I: *It sounds like a neat house to grow up in.*

P: It was. We had lot a fun. . . . You know, I would never want to live in another family. [Switches to a reflective tone.]

I: *Really? That good.*

P: I never said once that I'd want to be in a different family. I liked all the family we had. Somebody would say to my mother, "Why did you have so many kids?" My mother would say, "I don't know, maybe I should get rid of a few." And all the kids would look at her and say, "Not me!"

As can be seen in the preceeding interview, humor is often a prominent part of positive storytelling. This may be related to the fact that comedy is one of a few basic forms that stories can take. In addition, laughter often serves as a primer for other positive emotions. It provides an emotional release and a healthy perspective on life. As Lawrence Mintz observed, "Humor is the way we cope with living in an imperfect world with imperfect selves" (cited in Hafen, Karren, Frandsen, & Smith, 1996). Humor also provides a fail-safe empathic bridge between the storyteller and listener. Needless to say, humor in the context of the life narrative interview should be a primary goal.

The opportunity to focus on the positive will be missed if the interviewer allows the interview to gravitate toward processing painful past experiences, reviewing experiences of failure and loss, or discussing fears about the patient's current medical situation. These topics would be highly appropriate if the patient were in psychotherapy. Negative experiences and feelings play an important part in everyone's life and it is important to acknowledge them when they come up so that the patient feels accepted as a whole person. But in a life narrative interview it is important to move on to more positive experiences as soon as possible. In a practical sense, this means consistently focusing on topics that evoke positive thoughts and feelings for the patient. Discovering what there is to celebrate about the patient's life can be a joyful task for both storyteller and listener.

Here is a 45-year-old male patient (P) who had an unpleasant childhood and initially seemed to want to focus on it. The interviewer (I) had to work hard to maintain rapport and acknowledge the patient's experience, while at the same time shifting the focus to more positive topics. When the patient failed to take the cue to follow up on pleasant experiences, the interviewer deliberately changed the topic to a positive one (but without taking time to explain why).

P: I don't have very good memories of my childhood. It's kind of difficult to remember. I find that many of my problems are related to my childhood.

I: *Things weren't so great.*

P: Yeah. I was raised in a dysfunctional family. Although I didn't know it at the time.

I: *Hmm. [Sympathetically.]*

P: So I was kind of a loner as a kid and I don't really remember too much other than that I just kind of existed.

I: *When did things begin to get better?*

P: I got active in high school and I was in plays and things, and ran on the track and field team.

I: *Um-hmm. [Encouragingly.]*

P: Things got a little better and more enjoyable in high school, although I still felt like a loner inside. I didn't really know my own feelings and always felt different.

I: *Feelings in high school are so powerful.*

P: Right. I'm just working on feelings now.

I: *Hmm. [Sympathetically.]*

P: I think I was kind of numb through my life up until recently. So it hasn't been pleasant to go back and remember.

I: *[Changing tone of voice.] So, tell me what kind of plays you were in.*

P: Oh, mainly operettas. The Gilbert and Sullivan operettas. They were always fun.

I: *Wonderful—so you sang?*

P: Yes. . . . I played Major-General Stanley in Pirates of Penzance. That was a lot of fun. [Continues with positive memories.]

This example shows how tempting it would be to play the role of psychologist during the interview. This should be avoided. During the two research studies described in Chapter 3, several volunteers had a difficult time inhibiting their desire to be counselors rather than interviewers. During their first few interviews, they gravitated toward probing for feelings of hurt or conflict, rather than focusing on the positive. They then ended up offering advice or making supportive comments. While this effort was well intentioned, it does not belong in the context of a life narrative interview. Fortunately, most of these volunteers were able to change their approach, after much coaching.

Here's another example of how an interviewer can steer around potentially sad topics. This 70-year-old patient (P) was in the hospital for surgery and had been talking about his experiences before entering World War II. After hearing that the patient's wife had died recently, the interviewer (I) steered the interview in a very different direction than a therapist would have done by keeping it focused on the patient's experiences in the 1940s.

I: *You made some new friends in Carson City?*
P: Oh, yeah. Women.
I: *Oh? Is that where you met your wife?*
P: No. I met my wife in Maryland—my first wife.
I: *Uh-huh.*
P: We were married 37½ years. She passed away the second of January, last year.
I: *[Sympathetically.] Uh-huh. [Pause.] You've been remarried since then?*
P: Yeah. I've been married seven months now.
I: *Good for you. So, did you have a girlfriend back home when you left for the war?*
P: When I went overseas, yeah. I had one in New York. [Laughs.] I was engaged to her. We kind of broke up when I came back. We went together for about 2½ years.
I: *Do you remember your very first girlfriend?*

Any interviewer will occasionally be tempted to make a counseling-type comment when negative feelings surface during an interview. As in the previous examples, it is best to acknowledge these negative experiences briefly and then redirect the interview toward something positive. The same is true if the patient becomes tearful, as happens on rare occasions. The interviewer should acknowledge the tears by offering a tissue, give the patient a moment to recover, and then, with the permission of the patient, move on to the next topic.

GOAL 4: MAKE IT PERSONAL

To keep the storyteller engaged in a lively and personally meaningful way, topics and events should be personal and biographical rather than impersonal or informational. In addition, research by Haight (1992) has demonstrated that reminiscence interviews that focus on personal memories achieve more psychological benefits than those that focus on generational issues.

It is sometimes easy for storytellers to describe organizations they were involved in, how a particular piece of machinery worked, political issues or figures, experiences or opinions that many in their generation might have, or a variety of other topics that are not really personal. This can happen in deceptively subtle ways as well, as when participants tell interesting, detailed stories about events that happened to their friends or family but leave out their own involvement. The key is to bring the focus back as often as necessary to the storyteller's active involvement in the events of his or her life, and to the person's own thoughts and feelings about what was happening.

Here's an example of redirecting a 65-year-old woman (who was in the hospital for eye surgery) toward more personal details in her narrative. After a nice focus on personal recollections, she took a detour and started to discuss her views on the problems children have today. (P = patient; I = interviewer.)

> **P:** I was a cheerleader in high school. I went to all the football and basketball games.
> **I:** *What were your school colors?*
> **P:** Purple and white in high school, and blue and white in grammar school. They were some good days. I really enjoyed them. I always say now, if these kids were coming up today like we did, they'd be better kids.
> **I:** *Things were a lot simpler then.*
> **P:** Yeah. Kids today are different. There's all the drugs and violence. Gangs are in the schools in some places, and kids don't behave themselves. . . .
> **I:** *[Interrupts.] What do you think was a positive influence on your childhood?*

A similar problem occurs when some interviewees are too "intellectual" in their recollections, at the expense of reexperiencing the personal emotions linked to the stories. (Reminiscing, by definition, involves reexperiencing personal emotions.) While most individuals discuss the feelings that accompany their memories quite naturally, others have to be directed to do so. There are several methods for directing an interviewee to pause and focus on feelings associated with a memory. The simplest method is to ask the patient how he or she felt about the topic at hand. ("How did you feel about the holiday celebrations you had in your family?") If that leads to a one-word response without much reflection, then a second attempt might include an empathic statement to prime the interviewee's emotions. ("If I were in your shoes, I would have felt very good about how much you were able to do for your folks when they didn't have much money.") A final technique is to ask the person to elaborate further when he or she briefly mentions some feeling about a situation (e.g., "You said that your mother was a wonderful person. What did you like most about her?").

GOAL 5: FOLLOW THE THREADS CHRONOLOGICALLY

The storyteller's life is a complex tapestry of memories, and storytelling works best when you follow the threads of those memories in a simple, straightforward way. The best way to do this is to proceed chronologically, beginning with early childhood. In this way, the interview unfolds as a continuous life story rather than a series of unconnected anecdotes. Research by Haight (1992) confirms that the most salutary reminiscence interviews are those that proceed chronologically.

A variation on this is to proceed thematically *within* a chronological framework, questioning the storyteller about work, friendships, romance, and travel as the topics spin out naturally. This fits with a natural tendency of some storytellers, which was aptly described by one writer: "Historians often strive for a linear, chronological sequence; speakers may be more interested in pursuing and gathering together bundles of meanings, relationships and themes, across the linear span of their lifetimes" (Portelli, 1991; p. 63).

One 55-year-old woman hospitalized for cardiac surgery had a unique and interesting experience with her relatives. The interviewer (I) was able to help the patient (P) develop this more fully by following the thread of how it played out at different times in her life.

P: We used to have a "cousin club."
I: *You mean made up of all your cousins?*
P: Yes. All my cousins. We had about 12 of us.
I: *What did you do?*
P: We used to meet once a month at each other's houses. When it would be at your house, you'd make the dinner. And we'd put so much money in the pool. We'd play a game—a game of bingo—and there would be two prizes. Whoever won the first bingo and the second bingo would win the prize.
I: *Um-hmm.*
P: And every 3 months we'd go out to a nightclub or a show.
I: *It was just cousins? No boyfriends?*
P: Just the cousins. No fellows. All girls—just the girls. All women. We used to have a ball!
I: *[Matching her enthusiasm.] That sounds like a fun group.*
P: It was. We kept it up for 20 years.
I: *You kept it going even after you were married?*
P: Even later, when some people moved to Florida and some died.
I: *It sounds as though it kept you close as a family, too.*
P: Sure, real close. We have more pictures taken of the cousin club. [Laughing.] We really did call it the "cousin club."
I: *And you always knew what was going on in everybody's family, and with their children.*
P: Right. Right. We used to cook a beautiful dinner. You wanted ravioli, you'd make ravioli. You wanted something else, you'd make something else. You wanted sausage, you'd make sausage. Whoever was cooking would ask you what you'd like to have. So the majority would win.

I: *You mean you'd actually take a vote and the majority would win?*

P: Yes. This way we'd go see each other more often. Not just on a holiday or birthday.

I: *When you were little and growing up, the cousins would play together. But as you got older and everybody started to go their different ways, the club helped keep you together.*

P: Right. Right.

Sometimes an interviewer has an opportunity to pick up a positive thread that's been dropped and make a connection with a previous part of a story—as with this 67-year-old man, who was a diabetic outpatient. (P = patient; I = interviewer.)

P: My father ran a dry goods store for a while.

I: *A dry goods store—that's interesting. What was that like?*

P: Well, the store didn't do too well. It burned down. Came home one night and the whole place was gone.

I: *How old were you when that happened?*

P: Twelve years old.

I: *Oh, so that was at the same age you and your father won that car. [Refers back to an earlier part of the story.]*

P: Right.

I: *You went from good luck to bad luck. You had all the luck that year.*

P: Right. [Laughs.]

Whenever possible, ask questions that flow naturally from the topic at hand, and avoid abruptly interjecting new, unrelated topics. This frees the participant to tell stories as they unfold naturally from memory. When moving to another topic, look for a natural transition point. If an idea for an unrelated question comes to mind at a point where the interview is flowing well, jot it down on a notepad so you can come back to it later. This cuts down on interruptions.

In all cases, the thread you're following should end *before* you get to the present. Nothing gets a life narrative interview off the track more quickly than discussing an activity or situation in the participant's present life, which in many cases is likely to be influenced by the patient's current illness or limitations. This may be a fairly frequent situation, since after telling a story from the past the patient may naturally want to follow up with how that event has influenced his or her present life. For example, a storyteller might say: "After having that early experience of skiing I went on to become a regular at it. In fact, I'm planning a trip to Colorado this winter. I'm going to stay at . . . ." The interviewer should respond by redirecting the story-teller. (E.g., "I'd rather hear more about your teenage years, so we don't get off track."). The interviewer should also avoid the temptation to ask questions about the present. (E.g., "Are you still a skier?")

GOAL 6: GET THE BIG PICTURE

When an interview covers significant events from every important stage of the life span, the storyteller has an opportunity to integrate a wide variety of events. Presenting a broad tapestry of events adds weight and substance to the storytellers' sense of themselves. The difficulty in pursuing goal 6, though, is to avoid compromising rule 2 ("Show, don't tell") and thus missing the rich detailed images of the storyteller's life. There is a tension between the temptation to linger over and savor a few events in a person's life and to tour "17 countries in 3 days" and get at least a sketchy view of the complete picture. If you accept that neither goal will be achieved perfectly, the task then becomes to balance depth and breadth within the time constraints. This can be satisfying for both storyteller and listener. Our experience is that when the interview results in a relatively complete sketch of the storyteller's life, that also helps to keep the interviewer actively engaged.

GOAL 7: KEEP IT FRESH

Patients sometimes tell stories that seem programmed and stale. A patient who is the storytelling type and has often told stories about his or her past life may initially think that the goal is simply to do the same old thing on a larger scale. This is as tiring for the interviewer as it is for the storyteller. Even if the storyteller is drawn into telling favorite, often-repeated stories that appear to have a great deal of energy, such stories often fall into the category of performances of stock material. The interaction between storyteller and listener should create a fresh new story that actively engages and integrates past experience in a way that has never occurred before. When reminiscing is done from a fresh perspective, it brings experiences from the past back to life. Casey (1989) calls this the "revivifying" effect.

The goal for the interviewer is to evoke a lively, fresh, highly energized story rather than a rehash of stale old material. This can often be accomplished by asking a storyteller to focus on rarely recalled specific details and images, such as the smell and taste of a particular food or where and when he or she heard an old song for the first time. The interviewer can best do this by asking specific questions or making specific facilitating comments that evoke such memories from the storyteller's personal experience. This is particularly important when a story is about something the storyteller is likely to have narrated many times, such as meeting his or her spouse or serving in the army.

In the following example, the interviewer (I) picks up on a well-worn topic (cooking) and personalizes it in a charming and effective way. The patient (P), a 59-year-old woman, is then able to engage with the interviewer more energetically than would have been possible otherwise.

P: My grandmother would bake her cakes and pies on Saturdays and Sundays. I would just sit in the kitchen and watch her cook. Then we used to have a playhouse, and we would go out and I'd try to cook like I'd seen my grandmother cook. [Laughs.]

I: *That's neat. [Laughs with her.]*

P: But at the age of 9, I could cook as well as anyone.

I: *Could you? [With a tone of delight.]*

P: Yes. I could bake and cook as well as anyone, because I watched my grandmother. It was no problem. I watched how they cooked, and I had a talent for cooking.

I: *What was your favorite thing to cook?*

P: Let me see. . . . I'd have to think. [Pause.] Oh, I remember. That's easy. I loved to bake chocolate pies.

I: *Wow! [Laughs with her.] That must have been wonderful. Do you love chocolate?*

P: To this day, I love chocolate.

I: *Everybody in my family loves chocolate.*

P: To this day, chocolate pie is my favorite.

This is a good example of the power of a creative question at a key point in an interview. The interview might have progressed in a more pedestrian manner, asking the obvious questions. For instance, after "I had a talent for cooking," a less enterprising interviewer might have said, "You must have really enjoyed cooking." Similarly, there would have been less energy in the interview if after "chocolate pie," the interviewer asked, "What other kinds of pie did you make?"

GOAL 8: ENCOURAGE REFLECTION

Another approach to making the interview more meaningful for patients is to steer them toward being reflective, or philosophical. In essence, you are inviting interviewees to share some insights into life based on their real-life experiences. This is also known as wisdom.

When an emphasis on reflection is conveyed effectively, the interviewee begins to think automatically about and express the meaning of each event being described. For example, after describing piano lessons and practice sessions during childhood, an interviewee might conclude by reflecting that all this hard work was helpful because it instilled self-discipline early in life. A cautionary note, however: Care should be taken not to let the interviewee drift into transmissive reminiscence (see Chapter 2), which has the primary function of instructing the listener and tends to sound like preaching.

The most effective way to encourage reflection is to reinforce an interviewee who talks on that level. The interviewer can give reinforcement by showing increased interest, by nodding, or simply by asking the participant to elaborate further. Reflection can also be facilitated by questions that are provocative and stimulating. The following interview, with a 54-year-old patient hospitalized for knee surgery, shows how a simple question can trigger reflection. (I = interviewer; P = patient.)

I: *What made you decide to become a policeman?*
P: I always liked that. I always liked that type of work. I went into it for the excitement.
I: *Mmm, hmm.*
P: When you were a kid, you'd see movies. You see this and you see that. [Pause.] It isn't quite what you depict, in the movies. But, all in all, it's something different every day. In other words, I had no formal education. Just a high school education. And you go into a factory, and it's the same thing every day. I don't believe I could have handled that every day.
I: *No.*
P: And I liked it. I can never say I didn't like what I was doing. I still like being a policeman.
I: *I can imagine. You meet people, and you are doing some good.*
P: Oh, yeah!

In other instances, more creative questions are required to elicit reflection. Here are other examples of the types of questions that can be asked:

• What do you think motivated your parents to work so hard, day in and day out?
• When you were young, did your parents ever give you any advice along the lines of "Life is like a box of chocolates"?
• How did your religious faith play a role in your success?

- When you had your first child, what surprised you about being a parent?
- After having lived in both the country and the city, which do you think was the best place to raise your family?

GOAL 9: BE PREPARED

Finally, there is likely to be a point during almost every interview when even the most talkative patient gets stuck and doesn't know what to talk about next. Even the best storytellers can use an occasional cue from the interviewer to spark their memories. (E.g., "Tell me about the first car you owned") The interviewer should not read from a script—a set of written questions—but at such times it is crucial to be versed in a full range of topics that elicit positive recollections. Not having a number of such topics at hand can lead to predictability and a loss of interest and energy on the part of the interviewer and the patient. New interviewers should take time to study the list of topics and questions in Appendix B; these often lead to positive recollections of each stage of the life span. The interviewer can then facilitate unique and imaginative stories by adapting these questions and topics to the individual storyteller.

In the following interview with a 78-year-old woman with severe arthritis, the interviewer (I) elicited a series of positive recollections with a high-yield question. This question came at a time when the patient (P) was slowing down, not knowing what to say next.

I: What did you hear about your parents' journey from Poland?
P: My mother arrived in Buffalo by train, from Ellis Island.
I: *Oh, yes?*
P: Yes—my father went to Ellis Island to meet her. And she had her two little kids. My father came first to look for work. [To clarify the story.] He left her and my brother and sister back in Poland and saved up enough money to get them here. I wasn't born yet.
I: *Okay.*
P: So he went to the train station to meet them. She had my sister and my brother John, a little boy. And they didn't have suitcases in those days. She had pillows, family pictures, and everything wrapped up in sheets. They had her on the island, and they didn't let her go until he showed up. They didn't let you go until somebody came to pick you up.
I: *Is that right?*
P: When my father saw her, he couldn't get over it. She had so many bags.

You know, wide, big bags all tied up in a bundle. Sheets and pillows all hanging from her arms and a kid on each shoulder! [Laughing.]

I: *That's a great image.*

P: He said he was ashamed of her [Laughs.] But he wasn't. [Adds sentimentally.] He said, "She looked like an immigrant." [Pause.] She was!

I: *She was. [Laugh together.]*

P: All those pillows and everything. As if they didn't have pillows in America! [Laughs.] She didn't know.

I: *I guess you're right. How would she know?*

P: And then they all got on the train and they came to Buffalo. They slept on the train. It took 12 hours. They ate and then they got acquainted all over again.

I: *How many years had it been?*

P: He had been here about 3 years. When Stephie, my sister, first saw him, she said, "There's Daddy." And even little Johnnie said, "Papa, Papa." My father was crying like anything.

I: *He was?*

P: He couldn't believe that the boy knew him! He was so happy to be reunited with them. [Pause.] I also remember that my mother had sent a picture of herself with those two kids. She sent the picture from Poland to my father here.

I: *Before she came over?*

P: Yes. And so my father had a photographer put him in the picture with the family! [Laughs.]

I: *You're kidding me.*

P: No! No. It's still in the family. And he had another one made and he sent it to her!

I: *That's a fun story.*

REFERENCES

American Association of Retired Persons (1989). *Reminiscence: Finding meaning in memories. Training guide.* Washington, DC: Author.

Balint, M. (1964). *The doctor, his patient, and the illness.* London: Pitman Medical Publications.

Casey, E. S. (1989). *Remembering: A phenomenological study.* Bloomington, IN: Indiana University Press.

Hafen, B. Q, Karren, K. J., Frandsen, K. J., & Smith, N. L. (1996) *Mind/body health* (p. 548). Needham Heights, MA: Allyn & Bacon.

Haight, B. K. (1992). Long-term effects of a structured life review process. *Journal of Gerontology, 47,* 312–315.

Polster, E. (1987). *Every person's life is worth a novel.* New York: Norton.

Portelli, A. (1991). *Death of Luigi Trastulli and other stories: Form and meaning in oral history.* Albany: State University of New York Press.

CHAPTER 5

The Interview:
Beginnings, Middles, and Ends

I start at the beginning, go on to the end, then stop.
—*Anthony Burgess, novelist*

A life narrative interview, like any interview or story, has a beginning, middle, and end. In guiding a patient through a life narrative interview, interviewers need to be aware of the particular opportunities and difficulties faced by the storyteller at each stage so that the interview can proceed easily from beginning to end. In this chapter, we will review the skills and strategies that the interviewer can use to make the life narrative interview both enjoyable and effective at each step of the way.

BEGINNING THE INTERVIEW

Despite all the guidelines presented here on how to facilitate these interviews, it is worth remembering that storytelling is a natural process. Everyone seems to have a built-in sense of what it is to be a storyteller. This is particularly true for autobiographical stories: we are all capable of being fascinating oral historians when it comes to our own lives. Once the interview begins, the initial task is to guide the participant toward the natural role of storyteller. Storytelling, even under the best of circumstances, requires a certain self-indulgence and a focus on oneself. Modest people may find this process difficult at first, partly because it goes against the grain: the usual etiquette for everyday conversation is give-and-take. Moreover, in a medical setting the inhibitions against storytelling may be even stronger, because patients learn quickly that their caregivers are busy and don't usually have time for such things.

In a marriage, expectations about how the partners will interact with each other are often set during the first few weeks of the relationship. The same is true of the first few moments of a life narrative interview. In that time, two things should happen to establish the the patient's expectations and get things going. First, the interviewer should establish rapport, to develop an easy pattern of communication and minimize the inhibitions the participant may feel about disclosing personal information to a stranger. Second, the interviewer should explain the purpose of the interview and how to accomplish it.

Here's how one interviewer (I) achieved both goals with a 73-year-old patient who was in the hospital for a series of tests.

> **I:**   *The hospital is so strange. And there you are in a blue hospital gown. [Both laugh.] At home you'd be wearing something very different. So talking about home makes people feel more at home, and being reminded of nice memories makes people relax. So the idea of this interview is to talk about your life, and to begin, more or less, at the beginning. You've lived a pretty long life, and you must have some wonderful memories. What are your earliest memories?*

Before saying this, of course, the interviewer—a woman—had introduced herself and made some initial small talk. For patients in the hospital, asking about things that are likely to be personal, such as cards, pictures, or flowers in the room, is a good way to develop rapport and familiarity. For outpatients, other personal things, such as what a patient is wearing, can provide an opportunity to connect. Also, unlike what might happen in psychotherapy, a small amount of self-disclosure on the part of the interviewer, focusing on common experiences, will facilitate a sense of trust and warmth (this is discussed in detail in Chapter 6).

If the interviewer is not involved in the care of the patient, it is better to avoid asking specifically about the patient's medical condition. In our experience, if the interviewer starts by getting involved with the patient's current difficulties and concerns, this creates additional anxiety and makes it hard to switch gears and return to the point of the interview. Furthermore, it is a more positive experience for the interviewers when they can see a patient as an individual, rather than as "the case in bed A." In fact, this is the essence of the life narrative interview.

Once the preliminaries are taken care of, the interviewer should begin in a way that emphasizes the goals of the interview. For instance, here's how one interviewer began, with a woman who was awaiting surgery the next day.

> **I:** *We feel that reminiscing about early life gives real pleasure and puts people in a good frame of mind—which would be very helpful for somebody having a procedure like the one you're going to have. This may really help people get through it better. I think people's lives are very interesting, and I would enjoy it if you want to go into detail about things you like to remember. It seems to work better to do it chronologically, starting with the very earliest memories, and it doesn't really matter how far we get. What are some of your earliest memories?*

Here's one more example. After introducing herself and telling the patient (P, a 47-year-old woman with multiple sclerosis) how long the process would take, one interviewer (I) had the following exchange.

> **I:** *The idea of this conversation is that when people talk about their early lives—the happy events—it makes them feel good, and it's relaxing. That really is the main thing.*
> **P:** Okay.
> **I:** *So, if you were going to tell the story of Marie Smith [the patient's name] and begin at the beginning, what's the first thing you'd tell about?*
> **P:** You mean as a child growing up?
> **I:** *Mm-hmm. The very first thing.*

It is important to apply the best possible listening skills right from the start. A frequent mistake of inexperienced interviewers is to ask a flurry of questions at a fast pace during the first few minutes, before the interviewee has a chance to get comfortable in the role of story-teller. When this happens, the interviewee's natural reaction is to become more passive and to elaborate less. An expectation is created that the interviewer will ask questions and dictate topics at a fast pace for the entire interview. The interviewee needs to know at the outset that the purpose of the interview is *not* to learn as many facts as possible in an hour or less.

That being said, some individuals need more prompting and guidance than others to take on the role of storyteller. It is often useful to prime such interviewees with specific instructions. (For instance: "Tell me a story about what it was like growing up in your neighborhood.") Sometimes it helps to simply reassure a reticent patient that "everyone has a story worth telling." Another strategy for priming reluctant patients is to ask them to tell a story that they remember being told by a favorite relative when they were growing up.

Here's the beginning of an interview with an initially reluctant patient (P) who wasn't sure what was expected of him. Both interviewer and interviewee found it a bit awkward at the beginning, but the interviewer (I) kept encouraging the patient until he hit on a topic that piqued his interest and got him rolling.

I: *I'd like to talk with you about your life experiences and find out some of the interesting things you've done in your lifetime. Where did you grow up?*

P: Well, okay. I was born in Overton, Virginia in 1921.

I: *Uh-huh.*

P: Worked on a farm until I was 22, I believe, and then I went into the service.

I: *Let's go over some of that early stuff. I'd like to hear about your childhood years.*

P: Okay. Well, my father died when I was 11 months old. My mother married again when I was 5 years old. And we grew up on the farm, and all. [Pause.]

I: *You moved when you were 5?*

P: Uh, no. Yeah, yeah, we moved to his farm.

I: *Uh huh. You have any recollection of that?*

P: Uh, some, yeah.

I: *Some, huh? Was that the first farm you lived on?*

P: That was it, yeah.

I: *You have some recollection of it? What was that like?*

P: Well, you see, back in those days, they didn't have tractors. They had horses, and we plowed with horses. And we mined our own coal in mountains in the winter in Buckland County. We pulled that coal out with a horse and sled, for the winter, you know.

I: *Yeah.*

P: And we raised cattle, laid down our own livestock, and we had a water mill and ground grain for the whole community, you know.

I: *What did you have to do to run a mill?*

P: Well, okay. A water mill such as that is not very fast. . . .

In contrast, the following excerpt is from the beginning of an interview in which a patient (P)—a 38-year-old woman about to have minor surgery on her foot—immediately grasped the idea of the interview without much prompting. The interviewer (I) made an excellent facilitating comment ("Tell me a bit about your childhood") but then slowed the patient down with a closed-ended question based on an incorrect assumption. Fortunately, the patient took her cue from the original facilitating comment and went right into her story. The urge to tell one's story is a powerful one, and often the best way to start the interview is to simply get out of the way.

I: *You were born in Chicago?*

P: Yes, Oak Park. In the hospital.

I: *Mm-hmm. Tell me a bit about your childhood. How long did you live in Oak Park?*

P: Well, we didn't live in Oak Park. I was just born there.

I: *Oh.*

P: When I was a little girl, my parents belonged to a motorcycle club. There were about 500 motorcycle riders in the club, and they had an apartment building that they set up. . . .

THE MIDDLE OF THE INTERVIEW

Once the patient becomes engaged in the process and is comfortable with being a storyteller, the interviewer need focus on only two tasks: to *ask questions* and to *make facilitating comments* that implicitly pursue the process goals outlined in Chapter 4 without hampering the storyteller's spontaneity.

Many medical caregivers who have learned about techniques of interviewing medical patients may be familiar with the distinction between open-ended and closed-ended questions. Open-ended questions elicit more storytelling; such questions invite the patient to talk more expansively and personally about a topic for an unspecified length of time. (For example: "What was your neighborhood like?" "Tell me about your high school.") Closed-ended questions are used sparingly; they serve to clarify factual information that fills in the picture for the interviewer. ("How many sisters do you have?" "How old were you then?")

Both types of questions are obviously important. Closed-ended questions, however, need to be used with caution and mostly for purposes of clarification, because a closed-ended question primarily serves the interviewer's agenda, not the storyteller's. The goal is to ask such questions in a way that the storyteller experiences them as contributing to the storytelling process, not derailing it. For instance, if you've asked several closed-ended questions and note that the storyteller is waiting for you to ask another, you've asked too many. Ideally, any closed-ended question should signal to the storyteller that the listener is engaged and is trying to get the complete picture.

When an interviewee makes a transition from one period of life to the next, it can be helpful to establish the basic parameters of the participant's life at that time. This gives the interviewer a context in which to place the stories being told. For example, when the interview moves into young adulthood, the interviewer can ask whether the participant married or remained single, went to college, had a family, or had a career. It is also important for the interviewer to avoid unwittingly reinforcing any stigma that the participant may feel about not being "normal." This can be avoided by asking basic questions (e.g., "Did you ever get married?") before making any assumptions. It is critical not to imply any value judgments in the wording of the questions that are asked. Examples of questions that imply a value are: "You weren't a Nixon supporter at the time, were you?" or "Did you try to have children?"

Facilitating comments intrude least on the storytelling process and may be nonverbal (e.g., nodding or saying "Uh-huh") or more expressive ("That's really interesting"; "Tell me more about that"). Such comments acknowledge that the listener is attentive and sincerely interested, and that the storyteller is holding the listener's attention and interest. The implicit message here, of course, is that the storyteller is worthy of attention and interest, and of being taken seriously. The storyteller should perceive that message in every statement and question by the interviewer, because this perception will be one of the most important things the storyteller is left with when the life narrative interview is completed.

Facilitating comments and both open- and closed-ended questions can be used to steer the storyteller toward topics that the interviewer thinks might be important. The following interview was with a 55-year-old woman with back problems. Note the storyteller's response to the open- and closed-ended questions. (I = interviewer; P = patient.)

I: *Tell me about your favorite holidays when you were a kid.*
P: June 19th. My father worked for the Coca-Cola bottling company, and every year they would give a huge picnic for the whole family in Port Bolivar, Texas. They would charter buses and all.
I: *Is that on the coast?*
P: Yes. It's near Galveston, I think. But I can't tell you exactly where it is. [Ponders for a moment.] But anyway, every June 19th we'd go to the picnic. We'd always look forward to that. They'd pay for everything and furnish everything. It was maybe five or six buses just going down the highway. [With increasing delight.] We'd have a lot of fun.
I: *Sounds great. [Pause.] I'll bet you drank a lot of Coca-Cola.*
P: Yeah. Coca-Cola and all kinds of things.
I: *What do you remember having to eat?*
P: Let's see, what did we have to eat? Hot dogs. What else? . . . Oh yes, then all the men would go out crabbing. They would bring back a big net. We'd pick out all the shrimp, too.
I: *I'll bet you loved that.*
P: Yeah. They'd cook it right out on the beach.
I: *Neat.*
P: We'd play games and stuff with the other kids. We'd look forward to that every year.

I: *Were these kids you knew from the neighborhood or kids you just saw every year?*

P: They were families of the employees. So by going every year, we got to know them.

I: *That would be fun. Kind of like a reunion every year.*

P: [Enthusiastically.] Yeah, sort of like a reunion. [Pause.] I don't know if they still do that. Things have changed.

Here, the open-ended questions and some of the facilitating comments ("Tell me about your favorite holidays"; "What do you remember having to eat?" "I'll bet you loved that"; "Kind of like a reunion every year") opened doors for the patient and allowed her to be more forthcoming and enthusiastic about this positive experience. Unfortunately, the closed-ended questions ("Is that on the coast?" "Were these kids you knew from the neighborhood?") either tended to derail the storyteller's train of thought or were not responsive to what the storyteller had just said, letting potentially promising topics slide. As a result, by the end the storyteller was no longer actively engaged in the story and was thinking about it from her current perspective.

Keeping the narrative fresh and responding in a way that will promote the storyteller's enthusiasm are among the most useful process goals in the middle phase of a life narrative interview. When the interviewer is providing most of the energy and feels as though the process is hard work, not much happens, as in the following example. (I = interviewer, P = patient.)

I: *Did you have any favorite toys when you were a child?*

P: Just toys and dolls. [Pause.] And stuffed animals.

I: *Any favorite dolls?*

P: I did have a big doll, but she didn't fare too well. I think her arm fell off. Of course, this was when dolls were inexpensive.

I: *Were dolls your favorite toy, would you say?*

P: Probably, yeah.

I: *Did you have any games you'd like to play, like checkers or something like that?*

P: Ahh, I can't remember any specific game. I liked being with friends and stuff like that.

I: *Did you have a favorite friend?*

P: [More energetically.] I did, as a matter of fact, and she lived right next door to me. . . .

Here, the interviewer asked too many closed-ended questions about toys and dolls, questions in which the storyteller was uninterested. What did spark her interest turned out to be her friends. The interviewer might have discovered this earlier by asking an open-ended question such as, "What did you enjoy doing when you were a kid?"

By contrast, the following interviewer was more successful at facilitating the story of a 54-year-old man who was in the hospital for knee surgery. Notice how the interviewer's questions help the storyteller expand on his experience and avoid getting caught in a potentially negative topic. The interviewer (I) has framed even the closed-ended questions in such a way that they encourage the patient (P) to respond with more than a simple "yes" or "no."

I: *Did you grow up in Chicago?*

P: No. I grew up in a very little town. I'm sure you're familiar with it: Three Mile Island, the atomic plant?

I: *Oh, sure.*

P: About 8 miles from where that is. A cozy little town called Carlisle, Pennsylvania.

I: *Now, those nuclear plants weren't there when you were a kid, were they?*

P: No, no. There was a little island there. We used to get into a rowboat and go over to that little island. We'd swing on a tree into the river and go swimming there. No, they didn't start building the plant until 1955.

I: *It sounds as if you had an idyllic life, going out to an island in a rowboat.*

P: It was! Kind of like a Tom Sawyer thing.

I: *Yeah.*

P: Yeah, I had a very pleasant childhood. Like everybody else, we were poor.

I: *But you probably didn't know it at the time.*

P: No, we didn't. As a matter of fact, we were so used to it that we didn't really realize we were. Yet one thing was, we were never hungry. We always had plenty of food. [Pause.] But everything else was pretty scarce.

I: *Who did you row across the river with?*

P: Oh, my buddies. I had a lot of boys my age around.

I: *By the way, where did you get the boat?*

P: It was ours; we found it. About three times a year the river would flood and all kinds of goodies would show up.

I: *The flotsam and jetsam. [Laughs.]*

P: Yeah, we'd find all kinds of things in there. [Laughs.] We had our own little boat.

I: *[Encouragingly.] Um-hmm.*

P: And then someone gave us an old 5-horsepower motor. And then, oh boy, we were something. . . .

When patients have difficulty telling stories, it is especially important to go where the energy is. This means that when you are having a difficult time drawing a patient out during an interview, you need to be tuned in to topics that spark his or her interest. For example, one minimally talkative patient who gave only matter-of-fact answers to questions about his childhood finally showed some energy when he began talking about his favorite Christmas gift, a bicycle. The interviewer pursued this topic by asking specific questions about bike riding. This effort tapped into a lot of feelings, as the participant began to elaborate on the bike trips he would take with friends, what they would do, and who they would stop and see along the way. His bicycle ended up being the vehicle (pardon the pun) through which the participant was able to open up about his early life.

It is important, too, for the interviewer to feel engaged and energized. If the interviewer becomes bored, the storyteller needs to be directed toward a topic that both of them find interesting. Remember that the storytelling process is a creative interaction between storyteller and listener, and a crucial ingredient in a successful life narrative interview is genuine interest and enjoyment on the interviewer's part. Not all topics are interesting to all interviewers. If a patient is talking about his or her father's car collection in painstaking detail and you have no interest in old cars, gently redirect the patient to another topic.

ENDING THE INTERVIEW

Some warning should be given as the time allotted for the interview begins to run out. Very often, patients become so absorbed in the interview that they are surprised to find how much time has passed. A reminder can be given without much interruption to the process by combining a time check with a question or comment. For instance, a interviewer might say, "We have about 10 minutes left. What were your favorite things to plant in your garden?"

A time check allows the storyteller to sketch out the important facts that were not covered and to add any postscript to a story that was being told. For example, a participant might say, "By the way, let me tell you about that older brother who was always getting me into trouble. He ended up becoming a police officer." In addition, having some flexibility about the actual ending time allows the storyteller to reach a natural and unforced sense of closure.

It is best to end on a positive note with a summary statement by the interviewer about his or her reaction to the interview. For example, "This has been a delightful experience for me, and I hope you have enjoyed it as much. I appreciate your willingness to share some of the interesting experiences that you've had in your life." Another ending used by an interviewer was, "You've had a marvelous life so far, and it's been a pleasure and a privilege talking with you." Another comment was, "It was enjoyable for me, and I learned a lot."

As with all suggested statements, these are not meant to be "canned" or used verbatim. Interviewers should use their own sincerely felt words and add any other closing statements that fit into the spirit of the interview. The interviewer can add to these comments by reflecting on specific details or stories that captured his or her imagination, such as, "I really got a kick out of hearing about your adventures on the James River when you were a teenager. I'll think of you every time I see a kid paddling down the river."

These statements, even those referring to specific events in the interview, reflect not so much the content of the interview as the relationship that has developed between the storyteller and the interviewer. They express the interviewer's genuine respect of and appreciation for the storyteller, and the warmth of the connection between them. This is important in achieving the purposes of a life narrative interview—and very notable when it is absent. The following ending is relatively low on energy and is not very successful. (I = interviewer; P = patient.)

I: *Well, it has been very interesting talking to you, and I hope it gave you some pleasure.*

P: It did start me thinking about things I haven't thought about in a long time. And it did take my mind off all this medical stuff.

I: *Yeah. Well, I think it's going to go very well. You're in a good place for it. It's been nice meeting you.*

P: Very nice to meet you.

The point of the interview, of course, is not just to "meet" a patient or provide a distraction for a few minutes, although of course neither of those things is bad. The purpose of the life narrative interview is to give the patients something they can keep with them after it's over: a better sense of themselves, their personal resources, their caregivers, and their ability to deal with their medical difficulties. To achieve those goals, the interviewer needs to connect with and come to understand the patient in ways that the patient experiences as empathic and meaningful. The ending should reflect that experience.

I: *We're going to have to quit now. This has been such a pleasant experience. And I sure enjoyed hearing so much about your early life. I hope you enjoyed telling about it.*

P: Wonderful. It was beautiful. I feel real good.

I: *I want to tell you that I think you are a terrific lady. You're a lady who's had a*

*great sense of values in her life, and really knows how to make things work.
I wish you the very best.*

P: Thank you very much.

This is how we want patients to feel at the end of a life narrative interview: not just that it "takes their mind off all this medical stuff," but that they "feel real good." The most straightforward measure we have of the success of the storytelling process is that patients feel better. They feel better (and have less anxiety and a better sense of themselves and their situation) because they've connected with another person who has seen an important part of who they are and has come to understand them. They've also been reminded of positive aspects of themselves and ways they've handled difficult situations.

These effects cannot be faked, and they cannot be duplicated by a drug. They result from an interaction with a person who is comfortable and competent as an interviewer and who is willing to invest part of himself or herself in the process.

CHAPTER 6

Bringing Out the Storyteller: The Art of Effective Listening

The more deeply you listen, the more eloquently people will speak.
—*P. McLaughlin,* How to Interview

Good listening is the foundation of an effective life narrative interview. As noted in earlier chapters, the interpersonal exchange between the storyteller and the listener is essential to obtain the psychological benefits of storytelling. Regardless of how clever and creative your questions are, patients will get very little from the interview if you do not come across as someone who cares about who they are and what they have to say about their lives. In-depth listening is the primary way to convey this caring. As Mary Sarton observed, true caring shows itself by the quality of listening (cited in Gatz, 1989, p. 84).

On a more pragmatic level, the storyteller must feel connected with and affirmed by the listener in order to muster the energy that it takes to tell a story. Telling a story will be a draining experience unless the speaker is motivated by the listener. This is particularly true in the case of medical patients, whose energy is often limited. For these storytellers to invest energy in the story, the listener must also invest a significant effort in the process. The purpose of this chapter is to describe how to channel this effort into effective listening.

As easy as it sometimes seems, listening is a deceptively difficult art to master. All seasoned counselors know that the quality of their work with a client to a large extent hinges on the degree to which they are able

69

TABLE 6.1   Effective Listening

Attitude

    Mindfulness

    Nonjudgmental, affirming perspective

    Wonderment and appreciation

    Body positioning

    Silence

Action

    Empathy

    Self-Disclosure

    Summary statements

    Identifying themes

    Process comments

to discipline themselves to listen effectively. Unfortunately, listening is too often regarded as passive—as merely keeping quiet when another person is speaking. Passive listening may be appropriate at a movie or a lecture, but when we speak of listening in a therapeutic interview, we are not referring to something passive. Rather, we are referring to a type of listening that is much harder work, sometimes called *active listening*. This is a process that enables you to motivate and direct a speaker to think and talk deeply about a subject.

Developing the discipline of effective listening encompasses two different tasks (see Table 6.1). First, you must be able to attain the proper state of mind, or *attitude*. Second, you must master a specific set of active listening skills. We call this the *active* part of listening. This chapter deals with these two separate tasks.

DEVELOPING THE APPROPRIATE ATTITUDE

Several parallels can be drawn between effective listening and meditation. We therefore use the phrase *meditating on the speaker* to capture the attitude that is required for effective listening.

Jon Kabat-Zinn (1990), the author of a popular guide to meditation, begins his instructions by having students monitor their thinking and notice how most of the time they are not very mindful of the here and now. They are usually lost in thoughts about the past or future, and the present moment tends to get squeezed out. To illustrate this everyday lack of "mindfulness," he has students spend several minutes eating a single raisin, noticing nuances of sensation and taste that are missed when we eat in our usual way. Similarly, when we begin to pay close attention to our listening, we often discover that we are rarely fully present with a speaker. Instead, our thoughts are on either what we wish to say next or are distracted by topics that are tangential to the conversation.

Thus, as with meditation, becoming a good listener is an exercise in learning to focus and refocus our minds, again and again, as necessary. Like experienced meditators, good listeners learn to empty their minds of all other concerns and find the state of tranquility that comes from being fully present in an activity. In a sense, we are transcending our own personal concerns during an interview. All other elements of effective listening are predicated on being fully present with the speaker. The writer Henry Miller poignantly expressed the profound transformation that occurs when we focus exclusively on another person: "Everybody becomes a healer the moment he forgets about himself."

Adopting a *nonjudgmental, affirming* perspective is another important component of listening. This may be difficult at times, with patients who have values different from our own. Nonetheless, listeners must try to suspend value judgments and simply appreciate who the speaker is. The late Carl Rogers recognized the centrality of this attitude in building an effective therapeutic relationship. He predicated his method of psychotherapy, called *client-centered therapy,* on the concept of "unconditional positive regard" for the client (Rogers, 1951).

Similarly, an important part of effective listening is allowing yourself to feel and express a sense of *wonderment* at and *appreciation* for the unique experiences and personal qualities of the storyteller. Existential counselors refer to this process as "honoring" the patient's past. This is different from the clinical detachment that is often adopted by counselors and health professionals. After all, the patients are sharing a part of themselves that need not be understood or classified in clinical terms. Allow yourself to enjoy just being the audience. You, the listener, get the added benefit of being able to step out of your confining professional role during the interview.

As in meditation, *body positioning* contributes to the proper attitude for listening. Your body position will affect your ability to listen well. To paraphrase yoga philosophy: as the body goes, so goes the mind. For listening, this includes sitting in a comfortable, relaxed, settled position. Even small things, like opening your hands and resting them in your lap, make a difference. Similarly, your motivation to listen and your interest in the speaker are conveyed by what you do with your body, such as set-tling into a chair as though you were planning to stay awhile, leaning for-ward, maintaining good eye contact and an interested facial expression, and keeping a warm tone of voice. Too often in the medical setting, we talk to patients while looking down on them from a standing position. It changes the relationship dramatically when the patient and the inter-viewer both sit in a chair with their bodies positioned at the same level.

At the same time, the listener must pay close attention to the nonver-bal signals of the speaker to determine when he or she is uncomfortable with the topic at hand, is feeling excited about it, or is getting bored with it. The listener's facial expressions and gestures should be in sync with the feelings being expressed by the speaker. A videotape of a good inter-view should reveal a subtle dance, with the listener mirroring the non-verbal signals of the speaker.

Another common feature of meditation and listening is the importance of *silence*. People, in general, talk far too much when their intention is to listen. After years of training counselors and medical students through the use of audio- and videotapes, we have found a virtually universal truth. People who see or hear themselves conducting an interview on tape almost always say that they talked too much—that they didn't give patients enough time to think about what to say or how to say it. Learn-ing to stop interrupting begins with changing one's attitude about what it means to be a listener.

Allowing silences—pauses—when listening to another person is even more difficult to master than simply not interrupting. Unfortunately, most listeners become very uncomfortable after a pause of only a couple of seconds and feel compelled to fill the vacuum with another question or comment. Yet the amount of silence during an interview serves as an overall index of how comfortable the interviewer is with simply being with the person speaking, regardless of whether he or she is speaking at any given moment. Experts have noted that the number and length of pauses during an interview are highly correlated with the comfort and spontaneity of the interviewee—and that good interviewers allowed pauses of at least 4 or 5 seconds numerous times during an interview (Gorden, 1975; Sapira, 1990). As Gorden puts it, "Silence is as meaning-ful in verbal communication as rests are in a musical score" (p. 376).

Silences during an interview serve several functions. First, they pro-vide time for the speaker to collect his or her thoughts without being interrupted. Second, pauses send the message that the stage belongs to the speaker; the speaker can talk at his or her own pace, realizing that it's not necessary to ramble on just to keep the story going. Third, meaningful thoughts and reflections take time to develop; it also takes time to search for remote memories. Often, then, the most significant comments will follow a moment of silent reflection on the part of the storyteller.

Of course, knowing when to keep quiet and when to cue a storyteller is fundamentally important. As noted in Chapter 5, if you are too quiet at the beginning of the interview, some interviewees who are having difficulty getting into the role of storyteller may feel even more uncomfortable. Learning this subtle distinction will come with experience.

Again as with meditation, once the proper attitude is mastered, it can be more easily entered into whenever a situation calls for it. The listener no longer needs to struggle to get into the proper frame of mind.

THE ACTIVE PART OF LISTENING

Once the proper attitude is adopted, there are several skills listeners can use to convey that they are connected with the speaker. These skills constitute the *active* part of effective listening. Note that before describing these skills, we have first discussed the importance of the proper attitude. If we had reversed the order, it would sound as though *acting* like a good listener were more important than actually *being* a good listener. On the contrary, it must be remembered that the communication skills described in this section are valid only if they express things that come from our true selves, not stock phrases that we give on cue. In the words of Carl Rogers, the first and foremost duty of any healer is to be genuine and authentic at all times.

Empathy is undoubtedly the most important skill involved in active listening. Empathic listening involves true feeling on the part of the listener as well as communication; it is incomplete without both components.

Feeling involves to some extent stepping into the shoes of the other person to get a glimpse of what emotions the speaker was experiencing when the event being described occurred. This requires the listener to be attuned to the feelings that are underlying the stories.

Communication is a more difficult dimension of empathy. Even though many people are capable of empathy, they often are not skilled at communicating empathy to the speaker. When they are listening, they focus too narrowly on reflecting only positive feelings or they appear to be a blank slate. Expressing only what is positive usually does not reflect a full recognition of the speaker's true experience, and being a blank slate is only useful if you are a psychoanalyst. On the other hand, when empathy is communicated, either verbally or nonverbally, the narrator gets the message that you are listening so closely that you are able to mirror what he or she was feeling or thinking during the event.

Empathy is best expressed nonverbally, as by spontaneous laughter or a nod to show that you feel the emotion that has been expressed. However, in many instances explicit empathic statements are necessary. These are usually simple *reflections,* which are often left out in everyday conversation: "That really was a moment of joy," "That was a fabulous opportunity," or "Wow, what a letdown that must have been." To be effective, these statements need to be accurate and expressed in a tone that is congruent with the emotions of the storyteller.

When empathizing with a storyteller's feelings, it is important not to assume that the speaker felt a particular way if he or she is not conveying it to you either verbally or nonverbally. When you're not sure of the speaker's feelings, it is best to use the form of a question. For example, you might say, "If I were in that situation, I would have felt lonesome at first. Did you feel that way?" It is also important not to assume that a storyteller does not feel strongly about a topic because he or she is speaking matter-of-factly. Likewise, some individuals may need to be primed with an empathic statement to help them get in touch with their own feelings.

Although a transcript of an interview cannot capture nuances of tone of voice, the following excerpt illustrates the impact of subtle empathic statements. A 73-year-old surgical patient (P) was discussing being drafted into the army. (I = interviewer.)

> **I:** *How'd you get adjusted to being in the service?*
> **P:** I never did mind it too much.
> **I:** *Yeah? [Pause.]*
> **P:** You weren't by yourself. You were in there with thousands of other boys like yourself.
> **I:** *I guess you never felt alone.*
> **P:** Yeah, and after you stayed with a group of boys for 2 or 3 years, they're just like your brothers.
> **I:** *After a while it was just like being in a family. [The interviewer is remembering the patient's emphasis on his cohesive family earlier in the interview.]*
> **P:** Sure. Very much. You found people who would stand by you.

Carefully selected *self-disclosure* can also help you connect with a patient. When an opportunity presents itself, it can be useful to communicate the fact that you share some experience or feelings. This, in turn, invites the storyteller to describe the experience in greater depth. A disclosure might go as follows, "I was also raised in the south, so I know what you're saying about how people are different." An example follows of how a series of brief comments based on the interviewer's own experiences can draw out the feelings of the storyteller. This interview with a 48-year-old female patient (P) started with very little emotion. (I = interviewer.)

I: *What do you remember getting for Christmas?*
P: I can't really remember. [Long pause.] Except for when I got my first bike. I didn't see anything but that bike under the tree. I was about 8 when I got my first bike.
I: *Who taught you how to ride it?*
P: My sisters. It was red and white. I'll never forget it. I can see that red and white bike now. [Quietly, with a smile.]
I: *And you thought you were really speeding along. [Laughs, remembering her own experience riding her first bike.]*
P: Yes [With rising excitement.]
I: *And did your friends have bikes?*
P: Some of them did. We'd go for a ride together.
I: *Oh, that first bike. [Sighing.]*
P: That first bike is really something.
I: *Cruising around. Such a feeling of freedom.*
P: Yes, it was.
I: *Did you ride someplace where you bought Popsicles?*
P: Yes, we did. We rode to the store.
I: *And ride one-handed?*
P: No hands!
I: *Oh, the first day you can ride no hands.*

Of course, the interviewer does need to exercise some caution, so that the interview does not become a two-way conversation, where each person takes a turn talking. Although social norms dictate this kind of fair exchange, it has to be avoided in this context. In addition, care must be taken not to disrupt the flow or the continuity of the storytelling process.

The use of *summary statements* is another skill for conveying effectively that you get a point. These statements require the skill of seeing the main points within a story and then being able to paraphrase these points. For example, an interviewer might summarize a story by saying: "So you wanted to go to college, but your parents wanted you to continue to work in the factory because they felt that you were making good money." Summary statements send the message that you are connected with the storyteller and can also be used as a segue to get the participant to move on to the next topic. Sometimes this is necessary if a storyteller is spending too much time on one topic or is dwelling on something about which he or she has mixed feelings.

Similarly, it can be very effective to *identify themes*. This is a higher-level skill that separates the excellent listener from the average listener. Comments about themes work best when they are simple and to the point: "It sounds as though your childhood was filled with adventure," "Your family seemed to have a great deal of loyalty toward each other," or "It seems as if you have been very creative in the way you have accomplished things throughout your life." These kinds of comments can be inspiring for the storyteller because they indicate a high degree of active listening and they often put things into words that he or she has not used before. Moreover, as can be seen in the examples, a good listener often uses such comments to directly affirm a positive quality of the speaker.

The following interview with a 63-year-old woman facing surgery illustrates how the identification of positive themes can be very affirming and can evoke further reflections on the part of the patient. The interviewer (I) was commenting on the obvious family unity that partly grew out of living together in the same neighborhood. (P = patient.)

I: *Well, it sounds as if you had a warm and caring family—and probably still do.*
P: Yes.
I: *It seems as though you got a lot of strength from each other, and whatever came along, your family was there to give you support.*
P: Yes, very much. In fact, when everybody was in good health we used to help each other paint.
I: *Really?*
P: We used to paint my apartment, and when we got through we'd go paint my mother-in-law's downstairs. And when we got through with hers, we'd go paint my sister's down the street. [Laughing.]
I: *That's great.*
P: We'd support each other all the time. Same thing with the neighbors. We'd even dance outside together. [Laughing.] That's how close we were. And when anyone went to the grocery store, they'd always check with one another to see if anybody needed anything.

Last, active listening can be greatly enhanced by using *process comments*. A process comment is a remark by the listener about the conversation itself. For example, "You seem very enthusiastic when you are talking about your family." "We've been so wrapped up in this discussion that neither one of us has paid any attention to the time." This type of comment communicates the degree to which the listener is focused on the storyteller as a person in the here and now. In addition, such comments may help storytellers become more aware of the feelings they are experiencing as they become immersed in their stories. For example—

if the comment is accurate—a storyteller's awareness of his or her own enjoyment of the interview would be increased if the listener said, "As we've gone along here, your way of expressing yourself has become more and more creative and colorful." Generally, most professionals have some skill at making these comments when closing an interview, but they have more difficulty making them throughout the interview.

In this chapter we have described two components of the art of effective listening: attitude and actions. We have focused on some skills that are important for therapeutic listening in general, and on some that are specific to conducting an effective life narrative interview. These skills are important to review because most of us have fallen into bad habits when it comes to listening.

After reading this chapter, you may also be thinking that effective listening is a difficult art to master. While that is true, there is also good news: most experts agree that our listening skills can be greatly improved with practice and discipline. Feedback is probably the best tool we have for improvement. After an interview, we can ask for constructive feedback from the speaker, or we can ask a trusted colleague to review an audiotape. Since this process can be painful, it is important to ask for feedback on good points as well as on areas where improvement is needed. We can also learn a great deal by listening ourselves to audiotapes of our interviews. When doing this, keep in mind that almost everyone feels embarrassed and hypercritical when first listening to a tape of himself or herself.

Finally—once more as with meditation—we like to think of listening to a life story as taking part in something sacred. It can be a spiritually moving experience to embrace another person's life, even if just for an hour. This is particularly true when you are aware that only bits and pieces of an individual's life story have ever been shared before, as is the case for too many of us. An African proverb says, "Every time an old person dies, an entire library has been destroyed." Each interview, therefore, should be regarded as a precious opportunity to page through the texts of another person's life story.

REFERENCES

Gatz, M. (1989). Clinical psychology and aging. In M. Stovandt and G. R. Vanden-Bos (Eds.), *The Adult Years: Continuity and change* (pp. 79–114). Washington, DC: American Psychological Association.

Gorden, R. L. (1975). *Interviewing: Strategy, techniques and tactics.* Homewood, IL:
    Dorsey.
Kabat-Zinn, J. (1990). *Full catastrophe living.* New York: Dell.
McLaughlin, P. (1990). *How to interview: The art of the media interview.* Belling-
    ham, WA: Self-Counsel.
Rogers, C. (1951). *Client-centered therapy.* Boston: Houghton Mifflin.
Sapira, J. D. (1990). *The art and science of bedside diagnosis.* Baltimore: Urban &
    Schwarzenberg.

CHAPTER 7

Taking Life Narratives
to a Higher Level:
The Life Challenges Interview

We need to be reminded far more than we need to be instructed.
—Samuel Johnson

By following the methods and objectives outlined in Chapters 4, 5, and 6, any individual can conduct a basic life narrative interview. As noted in chapter 3, in the discussion of our research, we called this basic version the life experience interview (LEI). In this chapter, we will provide guidelines for a more fine-tuned approach to life narrative interviewing. For reasons that will be clear, we call this version the life challenges interview, LCI (Rybarczyk & Auerbach, 1990; Rybarczyk, Auerbach, Jorn, Lofland, & Perlman, 1993). We will describe how to add three objectives to the LEI to upgrade it to the LCI. Excerpts from interviews will be used to illustrate how these additional objectives can be accomplished.

OVERVIEW OF THE LIFE CHALLENGES INTERVIEW

The life challenges interview (LCI) is based on the simple premise that a life history interview which focuses on challenges successfully met will have a positive effect on the mood and appraisal processes of an individual facing a stressful event. Emotionally, the LCI is intended to increase patients' feelings of satisfaction, pride, and accomplishment with regard to their lives. Cognitively, the intention is to increase the individual's awareness of strengths and resources that were used in meeting past challenges. This awareness, in turn, will presumably affect the individual's appraisal of how capable he or she is of coping with any current medical stressors. Interpersonally, the intention is to provide the interviewee with a sense of affirmation of these positive qualities.

As noted in Chapter 3, our research showed that the LCI measurably enhanced coping, providing benefits over and above those obtained with the life experience interview (Rybarczyk & Auerbach, 1990; Rybarczyk et al., 1993). In addition to a decrease in anxiety, patients who participated in the LCI reported a greater sense of self-efficacy about their coping abilities, as compared with patients who had the LEI or were assigned to one of the control groups.

The LCI is essentially a life experience interview with three additional objectives: (1) reminiscing specifically about challenges successfully met (see the description of mastery reminiscence in Chapter 2); (2) underscoring the strengths and resources used to meet those challenges; and (3) summarizing key lifelong attributes at the close of the interview. Table 7.1 outlines these objectives, the methods used to accomplish them, and the specific outcomes associated with each.

Since the first requirement of the LCI is to accomplish the same process goals as the LEI, the initial focus should be on following the guidelines in Chapters 4–6. Only after the participant is in the proper storytelling mode can the additional objectives be pursued.

To keep the importance of the three additional objectives of the interview in proper perspective, we use a "75-25 rule." Roughly 75% of the time should be spent on the goals outlined in Chapters 4–6 and the remaining 25% on the objectives described in this chapter. However, this rule serves only as a general guideline, since no two interviews are alike and interviewers need to follow the flow of the interview to a large extent. As would be expected, in order to be successful at the LCI technique, more skill and more practice are required than for the LEI. Like a juggler, the interviewer should first become proficient at handling the basic goals before adding the LCI tasks.

The LCI should be introduced to the patient in the same way as the LEI, as described in Chapter 5. We have found that it is not worthwhile to try to explain the additional goals of the LCI, since an explanation takes up too much valuable time and can easily get bogged down in psychological jargon. Also, it can distract the patient from the natural

TABLE 7.1   The Life Challenges Interview: Additional Objectives

Objective	Method	Outcome
1. Reminiscing about challenges	Direct participant to focus on challenges	Feelings of satisfaction, accomplishment, pride
2. Underscoring strengths and resources in meeting challenges	Ask participant to identify or suggest strengths and resources	Heightened awareness of positive attributes; validation of positive self-concept
3. Adding a summary to the close of the interview	Summarize with participant key lifelong strengths and resources	Reinforcement of objective 2

process of telling a story by creating too many expectations about what should be covered. Remember that a key advantage of the life narrative approach to stress intervention is that it does not require the interviewee to understand how it works. The participant will become aware of the implicit goals of the interview as the interviewer shapes the storytelling with specific questions and comments. How to accomplish this will be outlined in the following sections.

OBJECTIVE 1: REMINISCING ABOUT CHALLENGES

The first objective of the LCI is to direct the interview so that the participant's life story highlights challenges successfully met. For the purposes of the LCI, *challenges* are broadly defined as situations, events, or circumstances in a person's life that called forth positive attitudes, abilities, skills, or resources. We chose the word *challenge* rather than *adversity* deliberately, to convey that we are focusing on things that were difficult to accomplish at first but eventually led to a positive outcome.

The challenges covered should be episodes that directly elicit feelings of satisfaction, accomplishment, and pride. In Appendix C, we have included an extensive set of questions that tap into challenges many people have met successfully during the course of their lives. These should be reviewed when you are first attempting the LCI, to get a sense of the range of topics that can be drawn on. This list is by no means exhaustive, however.

Challenges can be found easily in any of four general categories of life experiences: (1) developing a sense of competence and self-esteem (e.g., learning to drive a car, going on a first date); (2) achieving something that is valued (e.g., good grades); (3) making a transition in life (e.g., a new home, a new job); and (4) living in a time when there are fewer conveniences and resources (e.g., life before air conditioning, or life on a limited income).

The interview should avoid topics about which a patient is likely to have negative, unresolved feelings (e.g., anger or sadness). Examples of topics that should *not* be covered are tragedies, deaths, or any kinds of significant losses. Family problems should also be avoided, since they involve many complex feelings that take a long time to cover. The most important reason for not discussing these topics is that in any person's life story there is a potentially endless supply of other challenges successfully met.

We have also found that recent challenges should be avoided. It takes several years before one can look back on a challenge with the kind of wisdom that is encouraged in the LCI.

It is also inappropriate to discuss recent medical challenges. This recommendation is based on the fact that the interview is meant to be an opportunity to escape from, or transcend, current concerns and worries. Although the overall intention of the interview is to have the patient reappraise how capable he or she is of meeting the current medical challenge, it is better to let this happen implicitly.

It is not necessary to probe for challenges. Opportunities to talk about challenges will appear early and often during the course of a life story. In our research, a common mistake of newly trained interviewers was to search for challenges during the course of the interview. They would sometimes even ask directly, "Did you have any challenges?"—this would rarely lead to a productive response. The real problem, however, was that they were not applying a broad enough definition of a challenge. The most important skill to learn is how to slow down the interview enough so that when a challenge emerges, there is time to get the storyteller to reflect on it.

The following interview serves as an example of how the interviewer (I) was able to recognize two important challenges that the patient (P) had overcome in childhood and then draw out the stories connected with those challenges.

I: *How did you manage to have fun back then, without all the luxuries that kids have today?*

P: We were always doing something. We'd play hide-and-seek or something like that, you know.

I: *So you would have to be creative?*

P: We would always come up with something. Like walking in the woods. We had a lot of woods; we had a river down there; we'd go there and see snakes and throw rocks at snakes and things like that. We got a kick out of that. They had ponds. We'd go crawfishing and stuff like that. There was a lot to do over there.

I: *Were you and your friends afraid of anything that you can recall?*

P: Well, if you'd see a snake, you could get afraid of one, you know. [Laughs.]

I: *So you were afraid of snakes when you were young?*

P: When we saw one.

I: *How did you get over that fear?*

P: Well, I had a teacher in high school—he was a biology teacher. He asked us what you just asked me, if I was afraid of snakes. And he said, "Do you think you'd be man enough to take a snake up in your hands and hold onto him?" And I said, "No sir, I would not." And he went out and got a garden snake out of the grass and brought him in and said, "This snake won't hurt you. It's up to you if you want to be afraid of him. I don't blame you. But" he said, "this snake likes to be handled. You can make friends with it." So after that, I was never afraid of garden snakes. I'd pick one up. . . .

I: *So you ended up taking the snake? [Interrupting.]*

P: I took the snake in my hands and I said, "You sure he won't bite me?" He said, "He can't bite you. And besides, he likes the warmth of your skin. You'll have trouble getting rid of him." And he was right. I'd put him on the ground and he would crawl right back toward me.

I: *So you confronted your fear of snakes. A lot of people avoid what they're afraid of.*

P: . . . I'd forgotten all this stuff until you started asking me about it. [With a tone of satisfaction.]

I: *Well, that's what this interview is for.*

As the participant begins to tell a story about a challenge, the next step is to encourage him or her to be as reflective as possible about different aspects of that challenge. For example, a patient can discuss the difficulty that the challenge posed in the first place (e.g., "It was difficult to find a job in my hometown during the Depression because . . . "). A patient can also explore how he or she eventually met the challenge (e.g., "but somehow I managed to beat the odds and get a job by . . . "). Again, slowing down the interview and priming the storyteller with imaginative questions is the best way to encourage reflection.

Later in this same interview, the interviewer was able to stay with an important challenge and draw out the patient's reflections by asking questions from different angles.

I: *By the way, can you remember the first time you left home? . . . left your parents for a while?*

P: Yeah, my parents, I think, wanted to go on a second honeymoon or something. I didn't know it at the time, but they wanted to get rid of me for a few weeks, and they put me in a summer camp up here in the Appalachian mountains and took off for 6 or 8 weeks. And I had to go; I had no choice.

I: *That's quite a shock for a kid. It must have been frightening at first.*

P: It was. After a while, I got along fine. But then they came back to see me one time and that was the worst thing. [Laughs.] I started crying and jumping up and down, and I didn't want them to leave without taking me and all the stuff. If they had just left me alone and then gone, I'd have been all right, you know. But I got over that in a day or two.

I: *It sounds as though it was tough for a time there. It takes some getting used to not having your parents around.*

P: Well, they did that to me for two summers. I think it was good, because when I went off to vocational college, I was used to it. Otherwise, I'd have been in bad shape.

I: *So you made the best of that experience. You learned something valuable. . . .*

P: [Interrupts.] Yeah. I enjoyed myself at summer camp. The fact that my parents were leaving me—I thought they were never coming back, you know. I was 12 years old. That was it; they were gone. But after a while, all that changed. Everybody was my age at this camp. There were boys and girls in this camp. I enjoyed myself and even got a girlfriend. We played ball like we did in the neighborhood.

I: *You ended up making the best of it.*

P: And they had hikes up in the mountains. We hiked at a place called the Peaks of Otter. It was interesting, fascinating stuff.

I: *How did you feel about leaving at the end of the summer?*

P: Well, I was glad to go home, because I missed everybody at home. I was glad to see that my parents came back. When I looked back on it, I decided that summer camp was fun. When I went back a second year, I looked forward to it.

I: *Is that right?*

P: Yeah. The first time, I was scared to death. The second time, I looked forward to it, . . . but I still asked my parents, "You are coming back this time?" They said, "Yeah, we'll always come back, son."

I: *What do you think happened between those 2 years that made it more comfortable for you?*

P: Well, it was a positive experience. A real positive experience. It wasn't negative. That's what was on my mind.

I: *So you realized it was a good thing.*

P: Because there were times in the summer, you know, when we wouldn't have any school, and you got bored. Some days, there was nothing to do, nobody around, and I thought, "Boy, it would be nice to be back in summer camp." Because they had picnics, they had hikes, and you went up in the mountains. I had never been up in the mountains before. I had never seen anything like that except in the movies, you know. It was exciting.

As noted in Chapter 4, one of the most effective ways to encourage reflection throughout the interview is to reinforce the participant when he or she shares an important reflection. The patient (P) in the following interview was reinforced and encouraged to be even more reflective about the positive influence of her mother by the empathic and affirming comments of the interviewer (I). In this case, a 55-year-old African American woman was being interviewed by an age-peer female volunteer. The challenges are more subtle than in the previous example and relate to maintaining self-esteem as a young girl.

I: *Do you remember your first high heels?*
P: I never looked great in them. [Laughs.]
I: *Really? [With a tone of surprise.]*
P: I couldn't walk.
I: *Right. I know what you mean.*
P: Stumbling all over everything.
I: *But didn't you feel like a grown-up lady? . . . or trying to be one?*
P: Well, the first ones I wore were my mother's. And they were really high heels. [Laughs.]
I: *Spikes, huh?*
P: They were really high heels. So that was fun. [Pause.] I think I got my first pair at Easter. Yeah, Easter. Black patent leather.
I: *You must have looked just terrific.*
P: I thought so, whether I did or not. [Laughs, then switches to a serious tone.] Well, my mother, she always made sure that we looked good. She would always tell us how pretty we looked. My mother would always say, "Oh, you're so pretty." And we thought we were pretty. We thought we were the most gorgeous kids that ever lived. [Laughs.] We didn't know any better.
I: *Well, that's nice. [Warmly.]*
P: Because my mother would always tell us that.
I: *Well, sure, you are very pretty.*
P: We weren't selfish kids, but whatever my mother said, that was right. I mean her word was gospel.
I: *Right.*
P: She was a special type of woman. She really helped us feel good about ourselves. [Pause.] I can remember her now. She had these yellow pants suits she liked to wear all the time. And she had real long black hair. And she

would swish all around. She was the swishiest lady I've ever seen in my life. [Laughs.] Kids used to tease us about how much our mother swished when she walked.

I: *Really? [Laughs.]*

P: We used to feel kind of bad at times because they would tease us so much about it. But now, as I've gotten older, I've thought: well, hey, she had a graceful walk. [Pause.] But when she walked down the street, you did turn and look at her! That's the type of person she was. She really taught us to take pride in ourselves.

OBJECTIVE 2: UNDERSCORING STRENGTHS AND RESOURCES

Once the participant has gotten into the "groove" of discussing challenges successfully met, the interviewer should focus on the second objective of the LCI: underscoring the strengths and resources that allowed the participant to meet a specific challenge. The goal is to identify, reinforce, and validate positive attributes that are already part of the participant's self-concept.

Whenever possible, it is best to have participants identify their own positive attributes by prompting them with a question. (E.g., "What personal qualities did you have that helped you in that situation?") However, if the storyteller does not seem to be catching on, the interviewer can facilitate the process by making an observation about or reminding the patient of an apparent strength or resource. To emphasize how simple and straightforward these observations should be, we give examples in Table 7.2.

The process of underscoring strengths and resources should unfold gradually over the course of the interview. It is not productive to try to find a positive quality for every challenge that is mentioned. This would take too long and would interrupt the flow of the story. Also, during the early part of the interview, the interviewer should invite the participant to describe positive attributes without making any suggestions. If the interviewer asks questions about positive attributes, the participant will more than likely learn to think automatically along those lines, even if at first these questions do not lead to any clear answers.

The following interview serves as an illustration of how to steer an interviewee toward identifying positive personal attributes. This 55-year-old veteran of the Korean War began by discussing his success in training to be a paratrooper. The interviewer (I) then asked a few questions that drew out the patient's (P's) reflections about meeting the challenge.

TABLE 7.2   Examples of Statements about Strengths and Resources

"You've always been a resourceful person."

"You were willing to make a lot of sacrifices to achieve your goals."

"You really stand up for yourself when you need to."

"You seem to be very good at making adjustments."

"Your family really stuck together."

"The work ethic was very important to you."

"You have been good at finding creative solutions to things."

"Your willpower got you through again."

"Your sense of humor served you well."

"You seem to have had lots of love in your life."

Note: These comments can be stated in the present tense or past tense.

P: On about the third day I was in the army, they asked for volunteers to be paratroopers. I asked, "What have you got to do to be a paratrooper?" The guy showed us movies of paratroopers jumping out of planes. After he left, the sergeant looked at me and said, "You really want to know what you got to do to be a paratrooper?" I said "Yeah." He said, "You've got to be an idiot." So I joined. [Both laugh.] They sent me to Fort Campbell, Kentucky, for basic training the next week.

I: *So you didn't let fear stop you?*

P: No. I wasn't afraid. I really wanted to know what it was like to jump out of an airplane.

I: *Sure.*

P: The fear came when it was time to jump out of the plane. [Laughs.]

I: *Naturally. But how did you get as far as getting into the plane in the first place?*

P: Well, they trained us and trained us and trained us. They trained us for 3 weeks. They made us go up a 34-foot tower with a strap and a rope on our backs. That scared the daylights out of me. You jump and almost hit the ground. The strap catches you just in time. You were yanked back up and went on down a cable until you hit a pile of sawdust.

I: *Wow.*

P: And once I did that a dozen times, I looked forward to getting into the airplane. [Both laugh.]

I: *They broke you in gradually.*

P: After you've been up a few times, then really there's nothing to it after that.

Next, the interviewer asked the patient to label his positive qualities. When the patient seemed not to be addressing the question directly, the interviewer offered an observation based on earlier stories (i.e., "Determination?"). The patient later adopted the label that was suggested to him, almost as though it were his own word.

I: *What personal assets did you have that made it all right for you?*
P: I don't know.
I: *Take a guess.*
P: [Pause.] I just wanted to be a paratrooper, that's all. I wanted to be somebody. To me that was great. That's how I got through it, I think . . .
I: *[Interrupts.] Determination?*
P: . . . otherwise, running 4 miles before breakfast every day and doing 50 push-ups. [With increasing excitement.] I couldn't do 50 push-ups. I could do 25 and fake the other 25. I think that all paratroopers, the same as all marines, we were determined to be it. You could flunk out, you know, . . . or you could get through. If you could get through, you were a success. Some of my buddies couldn't run very far, but I could run. I drank a lot and smoked a lot too. But I could run, run, run. Some of them couldn't; they'd get sick to their stomach. The sergeant would see them and say, "Do you want to be a paratrooper?" The guy would say, "Yeah." He'd be sick to his stomach and couldn't run any more. And the sergeant would pick him up off the ground and drag him back. They'd pull him back on their shoulders. And that was something I really admired and respected them for.
I: *Yeah.*
P: They said if the guy really wanted to be a paratrooper, he was going to be one. And they'd drag him back in. Whether the guy could walk or run, or not, it didn't make any difference.
I: *Yeah.*
P: So I was determined to be one. That's the only reason I got to be one.

The interviewer should not be concerned if patients shy away from naming their own positive qualities when directly asked. Many participants simply need to get warmed up before they feel at ease talking about their strengths and resources. However, some participants continue to have a difficult time acknowledging their personal strengths. They simply will not brag about themselves. In most of these cases, there is an awareness of a positive ability, but the person does not wish to verbalize it in the interview because of shame or embarrassment about being immodest, even for a brief moment. In some cases, when the interviewer verbalizes a positive ability, the patient is then able to acknowledge it with a sense of pride.

In most cases, it is only after the interviewer has established rapport and there has been time enough to recognize themes in the life story that observations about positive personal attributes can be offered. The following well-supported statements by one female interviewer (I) near the end of an interview were favorably received by the 53-year-old female patient (P).

> **I:** *I notice that you really like to take on new challenges. You just decided you wanted to learn to jitterbug and went for it. You also approached learning to knit and your move to Chicago in the same way.*
>
> **P:** That's true. [Pause.] I never thought of it that way before.
>
> **I:** *Even when you were a kid, you just made up your mind that you were going to climb that tree and did it.*
>
> **P:** Sure. I wasn't gonna let my brother show me up.

Other individuals, when asked, avoid taking direct credit for the positive events in their life by attributing these to a blessing from a higher power or just plain good luck. With these individuals, further probing will sometimes lead to an acknowledgment of a positive quality. For example, when asked, "How did you manage to do so well in your business?" one interviewee replied, "Just good luck, I guess." The interviewer was then able to get the participant to identify positive attributes by prompting him with a question: "Don't you think you have to make your own luck? Not everybody gets that lucky."

Finally, it is also useful to look for events that capture the *essence* of the participant's strengths and resources. Those events can later be referred back to as "touchstones." During the rest of the interview, parallels can be drawn between the strengths and resources that emerged during these touchstone stories and other events being described. During an interview with a 58-year-old female cardiac patient (P), the following exchange took place, beginning with a creative question from the interviewer (I).

> **I:** *As a kid, did you make trips to Lake Michigan? Did you go swimming on the beaches? [The interviewer is referring to a popular pastime for residents of Chicago.]*
>
> **P:** Well, we weren't allowed to go the beach.
>
> **I:** *That was too far for you, I guess?*
>
> **P:** Our father didn't want us to be in a bathing suit. But when we got a little older, we decided to sneak out there.
>
> **I:** *Ah-hah. [Both laugh.]*
>
> **P:** The one time we did it, some guys came along and actually stole our clothes. The first time we did it!
>
> **I:** *Oh, no. What did you do?*
>
> **P:** So we borrowed clothes from people that were out there. Some people that were there gave us a coat and some shoes. Any they gave us money to take the streetcar home. All the money we had was stolen.
>
> **I:** *Oh, my goodness. That was quite an experience!*

P: So when I went home, I had to sneak in. My friend had to sneak in and get my apron and bring it back to me so my father couldn't see what I had on. . . . You weren't allowed to go to the beach.

I: *What happened when your parents found out?*

P: Well, my mother, she was a softie. It was my father I had to worry about. He never found out.

Much later in the interview, when discussing how the patient persevered and eventually quit smoking after several tries, the interviewer made the following comment.

I: *Well, you are a woman of great determination. After all, you got back from the beach without any clothes. [Laughs.]*

P: That's true, I am. [She goes on to discuss another incident where she showed determination.]

People always have a few favorite stories that serve to remind them of their strengths and their resources for meeting challenges. The events described often took place during turning points or "defining moments" of a person's life. These stories are frequently retold when the individual is in the midst of a stressful situation. For example, men who served in World War II often tell war stories when they are facing a challenging situation, to remind themselves and others that they are competent. That's why we often refer to our stories of overcoming challenges as "war stories."

OBJECTIVE 3:
SUMMARIZING STRENGTHS AND RESOURCES

The final few minutes of the LCI should be used to accomplish the goals outlined in the section on "Ending the Interview" in Chapter 5 and to summarize the strengths and resources that have emerged from the life story. The objective of this part of the interview is to reinforce the positive aspects of the patient's self-concept and coping strengths that were brought out during the interview. This can be accomplished in different ways.

One approach is to have the interviewer provide a wrap-up of the positive themes that were brought out during the interview. To do this, the interviewer needs to keep track of these strengths and resources. This type of wrap-up is most effective when it is concise and covers two or three primary strengths and resources. Again, the emphasis is on simple, straightforward observations. This summation can be posed in question form, as in the following statement.

> **I:** *It seems to me that a main source of strength in your life during challenging times has been your spirituality and your creativity. Would you agree with that?*

These summary observations can also be combined with the usual closing comments about appreciating the participant's willingness to share his or her memories and the interviewer's enjoyment of the interview.

> **I:** *It's been a pleasure and a privilege hearing about your life experiences. You've had a very blessed and successful life. I am particularly impressed with your ability to take advantage of good opportunities when they come along and the family support you have received throughout your life. You also have a knack for coming up with creative solutions to challenging situations.*

However, the easiest and best way to reinforce the self-concept is to ask the interviewee to summarize his or her life story in some way. If there is consistent emphasis throughout the interview on positive aspects of the self-concept and resourcefulness that were manifested during important life events, often the storyteller will provide an inspired and elegant summary. Such was the case in a moving interview with a 72-year-old African American woman awaiting coronary artery bypass surgery. She had endured much poverty in her life. (I = interviewer; P = patient.)

> **I:** *How would you like to sum up your life in a couple of words?*
> **P:** I would say it has been a good life. [Hesitating.] But money plays a big part in your life, and I really didn't have much money.
> **I:** *Mm-hmm.*
> **P:** I was pretty poor. But it was a happy poor, I would say. I was happy. For what I did have, I was happy. Because whatever I did have, I made the best of it!
> **I:** *I get that impression, that you make the best of any kind of situation you're in.*
> **P:** What I did have, I made the best of it. Yes, I just didn't worry over what I didn't have. Or what I "need" to have. Or what I wanted! [Pause; changes to a more reflective mood.] So that's what I can say. I don't know much more I can say about my past life.
> **I:** *That says a lot.*
> **P:** It was difficult for my generation [Referring back to her earlier comments about how hard it was in Mississippi when she was growing up.] . . . But I have no regrets.

I: *Well, I hope this interview has helped you think about the good things in your life again.*

P: You know, I can think of these memories on my own. But for me to go all the way back, and do like this interview. . . . You know, I never did this before. To me, now I can see, since talking to you, that my life wasn't a failure or wasn't, you know, a disgusting life. [Emphatically.] I would say I did have a good life. I would say a rich life!

I: *Sounds like it.*

P: I had good health. Strong. Strong health and a strong mind! When you 've got that, you've got everything.

I: *Sure have. [Pause.] Well, thank you very much. [Draws the interview to a final close.]*

P: It's been good to go back. Thank you.

REFERENCES

Rybarczyk, B. D., & Auerbach, S. M. (1990). Reminiscence interviews as stress management interventions for older patients undergoing surgery. *The Gerontologist, 30,* 522–528.

Rybarczyk, B. D., Auerbach, S. M., Jorn, M., Lofland, K., & Perlman, M. (1993). Using volunteers and reminiscence to help older adults cope with an invasive medical procedure: A follow-up study. *Behavior, Health, and Aging, 3,* 147–162.

CHAPTER 8

Practical Issues

God is in the details.—Ludwig Mies Van der Rohe

There are a variety of opportunities in the medical setting for using the life narrative interviews described in this book. Before you can use them, however, there are numerous practical issues to consider. These include whom to interview, when and how to conduct the interview, how to interview different types of patients, how to preserve confidentiality, and how to evaluate the effectiveness of the interview. Addressing these issues before you start can help ensure a satisfying and successful interview.

WHAT KIND OF PATIENT SHOULD BE INTERVIEWED?

This is a trick question. In essence, the real question is: What kind of people want to tell their story, be known for who they are, receive respect and acknowledgment for their accomplishments, and have someone celebrate their joys and experiences? The answer, of course, is everyone.

In a practical sense, however, we make choices about whom we offer a life narrative interview when it is used as a specific intervention. These choices are not as hard and fast as those related to ordering a course of biomedical treatment, because key elements of life narrative interviewing can be a part of any interaction with a patient. In that sense, we can think in terms of two types of interviews.

93

First, there are *impromptu* interviews that are conducted as part of regular contact with a patient (e.g., while providing nursing services). As with a more formal interview, when an opportunity to hear about a patient presents itself, we make choices about how attentively we listen, how we respond to the patient's stories, and whether or not we cut him or her off and go on to other things. Although the choices we make may or may not be conscious, they have consequences. We let patients know unmistakably whether the part of themselves they share with us is important. Dismissing a patient's story, even a brief one, is a lost opportunity to connect with the patient and create positive psychological and possibly even medical benefits.

Second, there is the *scheduled* life experience interview or life challenges interview, in which a specified length of time set is aside solely for this purpose. This chapter takes up practical issues of scheduled interviews.

Because of the additional investment of time and effort required to conduct an LEI and an LCI, they should be used selectively with patients who are facing high levels of stress. Fortunately, life narrative interviews can be adapted to a wide variety of stressful situations. First, the interview can be used as a coping resource offered to patients at critically stressful points. For instance, patients can be offered a life narrative interview before an MRI or surgery, during chemotherapy or kidney dialysis, or after a disabling medical event (e.g., an amputation or a hip fracture). Second, LEIs or LCIs can also be administered as a regular part of the medical service for patients who appear to be stressed or anxious. For example, interviews can be scheduled with cancer patients who appear to be significantly stressed or anxious because of their illness.

As we have noted before, these interviews are not a sufficient intervention for individuals suspected of having a bona fide psychological disorder. But for patients who may be reluctant to deal with their stress directly, life narrative interviews appear to be an ideal intervention. One key to their effectiveness may be that they can be presented as an inherently enjoyable opportunity to tell one's life story and as something that may improve one's state of mind. In effect, individuals can participate without acknowledging that they are in need of psychological assistance. Life narrative interviews can therefore be useful with a wider range of patients than more formal interactions (e.g., relaxation training).

This is undoubtedly one of the reasons they are so effective for older adults, who are often reluctant to participate in traditional psychological interventions (Brody, 1985) and for whom multisession reminiscence sessions aimed at both short-term and long-term psychological benefits have been shown to be effective (Haight, 1991). For similar reasons, life narrative interviews should provide benefits for younger adults who are adjusting to life-threatening illnesses such as cancer or AIDS, as illustrated by Borden (1992) and our first clinical vignette in Chapter 1.

INTERVIEWS: HOW LONG AND HOW MANY?

Life narrative interviews can be given either once or as a series. A single interview is best when the patient is facing a circumscribed medical procedure, while a series of interviews may be well suited to a patient who is undergoing a long-term medical procedure that requires an extended coping effort. For instance, we collaborated on designing a program that would provide a series of life challenges interviews (LCIs) to patients undergoing hemodialysis.

A one-time interview that takes place immediately before a stressful medical experience must be fitted into the other demands on the patient's time. These demands include medical tests and examinations, visits by physicians, sleep, meals, family visits, and time to be alone. Given these practical limitations, we have found that 45 minutes to 1 hour is about the optimal duration for one interview. The quality of the interview and the degree to which the participants can stay focused seem to diminish when the time is lengthened. Conversely, when the interview is shortened, it often feels rushed.

A series of interviews may be more effective with patients who are coping with more protracted medical procedures. These procedures would include chemotherapy treatments for cancer patients and hemodialysis for patients with kidney failure. In some instances, the interviews could be conducted while the patient is receiving the treatment. For this type of interview, the patient would participate in three to six 45-minute sessions. If it seems appropriate, each interview session can be planned to cover a specific period in a person's life so that by the end of the series the patient's entire life story is covered.

We believe that multiple interviews are often more effective than single interviews in facilitating patients' adjustment, and they have advantages for the interviewer as well. As a more in-depth process, multiple interviews encourage patients to think about the positive aspects of their lives. The interviewee also has time between sessions to contemplate the events that were discussed and to think ahead about topics to bring up next time. Meanwhile, the interviewer can listen to an audiotape of the previous interview and get ideas for follow-up questions and changes in the approach used with the patient (see the discussion of audiotaping later in this chapter). A peer or supervisor can also listen to the audiotape and provide constructive feedback.

WHO SHOULD CONDUCT LIFE NARRATIVE INTERVIEWS?

Life narrative interviews can be conducted effectively by health professionals or volunteers without extensive training in counseling. Interviews can be provided by hospital staff members who address the psychological needs of patients as part of their role (e.g., nurses, recreation therapists, social workers, psychologists, chaplains); by those who are able to spend additional time with patients (e.g., medical students or nursing students); or by volunteers who have an interest in interacting with patients. (Chapter 9 covers the use of volunteers in more detail.) For professionals who are considering conducting a life narrative interview, the most important factor is whether or not there is time to fit it in with other professional duties.

Elements of life narrative interviewing can be incorporated into any interaction with patients. Patients frequently want to talk about their past as a way of saying who they are and what is important to them. Too often, professionals consider this part of the conversation a distraction and half-listen until they can politely change the subject. Instead, these instances can be viewed as an opportunity to employ the interviewing techniques described earlier, even if only briefly. Furthermore, some professionals will have opportunities to conduct a formal life narrative interview. Nurses, nurse's aides, social workers, psychologists, recreation therapists, and chaplains will probably have more opportunities, while physicians may have fewer chances. Nonetheless, on the basis of our experience training medical students and residents, we would say that physicians can be very effective at working life narrative interview techniques into their contacts with patients.

Acute care physicians often see patients repeatedly over a substantial period of time. Oncologists, cardiologists, and other specialists need to know something about their patients' lives and coping resources in order to help them make choices about treatment and deal with psychosocial issues. They may be able to briefly incorporate elements of life narrative interviews in each of their interactions, to get to know their patients better over time and assist them in dealing with the stress and anxiety associated with their illnesses. Such interactions may also contribute significantly to the sense of caring and reassurance that the patient feels, which has a beneficial effect in itself. Some parts of life narrative interviewing will be more relevant than others, of course. Undoubtedly, in many cases it will be more useful to talk briefly with patients about how they've dealt successfully with other stressful situations than about their memories of their high school prom.

Primary care physicians may be able to use these interviews over a period of time when building a relationship with their patients. Although life narrative interviewing would be difficult to accomplish in a practice where each patient is seen for only 10 or 15 minutes, elements can be appropriate for primary care physicians who schedule longer sessions to get to know new patients or to deal with more involved issues. This is particularly true for the large number of patients whose health concerns involve a great deal of anxiety or distress. As described previously, portions of life narrative interviews, particularly the life challenges interview (LCI), may be the most appropriate for patients who come in frequently, are experiencing distress from their medical problems, or are having difficulties adhering to their treatment regimen.

Additionally, psychiatrists or other therapists who counsel medical patients may find it useful to encourage patients to tell stories about positive past events and coping strategies for the purpose of reducing their symptoms of anxiety or reactive depression. As psychologists, we have used elements of life narrative interviewing in both outpatient settings and inpatient consultation-liaison settings. We have found it to be a particularly useful adjunct to the care of several categories of patients: those who are unwilling to learn the exercises involved in cognitive-behavioral therapy for anxiety, those who are unable to do the exercises because of cognitive deficits affecting concentration (but not verbal ability or long-term memory), and those who are suspicious of therapy but may be willing to talk about relatively safe topics from their past.

WHAT HAPPENS BEFORE THE INTERVIEW?

The interview is like a performance, and it is important to set the stage. In an inpatient setting, this begins before the interview by scheduling to minimize the likelihood of interruptions or distractions, such as visits from physicians or family members. Sometimes the hospital will have a private conference room available on each unit that can be used. Otherwise, advance preparations should be made that help ensure the patient's privacy (e.g., checking with the nurse and physician just before the interview to see if medications can be given or vital signs can be taken in advance).

Before starting the interview, the interviewer may need to ask visiting family members politely to "take a break and get a cup of coffee." It should be explained that the interview is most effective when it is a solo experience, and if they are curious they can ask the patient after the interview for a copy of the audiotape. If they insist on being present, they can be asked to be part of the audience rather than act as additional participants. Ideally, the phone should be taken off the hook. If a roommate is present, the curtain should be drawn between the two beds, serving as a signal that the conversation is private. In addition, the interviewer should find a comfortable chair that can be pulled close to the patient and positioned at a comfortable distance from the patient. When storytelling takes place, there is usually a more intimate distance between the listener and storyteller than is typical in everyday conversation.

This setup time is also the appropriate point to secure permission to audiotape the interview. As noted previously, almost all patients respond positively to having the interview recorded. It seems to add a sense of importance and drama to the interview, a kind of recording of one's life for posterity. Even if the patient immediately consents to audiotaping, however, it is still important to discuss your policy concerning confidentiality (see the discussion later in this chapter). Make it clear to the patient that the tape will be used for supervision purposes only and will not be shared with anyone else unless permission is obtained. Since interviews often turn out so well, it is not uncommon for participants to ask for copies of the tapes. Of course, these should be provided. When a family member requests a copy, the interviewer should ask the patient for permission in private, when the family member is not present.

A note of caution. If the audiotaping fails, it can be very disappointing to both you and the patient. Test the recorder before the interview begins by recording a few seconds of dialogue, rewinding, and playing it back. Some patients who have limited energy tend to speak quietly. Be sure the microphone is close enough to pick up the patient's voice. Also, be very careful if you are turning a tape over in the middle of the interview. It's easy to record over the side you've just finished. Immediately after the interview is finished, the tape should be labeled with the patient's name and the date and the tabs should be removed so that it can't be taped over accidentally.

WHAT ABOUT AGE DIFFERENCES
BETWEEN INTERVIEWERS AND PATIENTS?

While everyone agrees that a good interview can take place between individuals of any ages, there is debate as to which is the better combination, age-peer interviewers or cross-generational interviewers. As we've already discussed, our research indicates that age-peer interviewers are no more effective than interviewers of a different generation—except in the life challenges interview, where age-peers had a significantly more positive effect on patient's coping self-efficacy beliefs than cross-generational interviewers. We hypothesized that the better performance was related to the fact that the age-peer interviewers had lived through the same time period and could directly relate to many of the events, challenges, and accomplishments described by the patient. The interviewer's affirmation of the patient's accomplishment in meeting life challenges would therefore have greater credibility and meaning. A greater level of kinship, trust, and openness between members of the same generation may also play a role.

However, we want to emphasize that the effectiveness of any given interview is determined primarily by the efforts and skill of the interviewer. Skillful interviewers often find ways to use a lack of comon experience to their advantage. For example, a younger interviewer might encourage an older interviewee to be more descriptive by saying "I can't imagine what it was like to live through that time. Can you give me a sense?"

IS GENDER A FACTOR IN THE INTERVIEWS?

Several writers have recently suggested that men and women communicate and tell stories differently (Gray, 1992; Tannen, 1990; Webster, 1995). While some authors contend that women's stories have been "largely untold and unheard" in our culture (Laird, 1989), two studies have found that women of all ages report reminiscing more frequently than men (Merriam & Cross, 1982; Webster, 1995). Webster also found that women and men reminisce for different reasons.

It is easy to overstate the differences between the communication styles and goals of men and women. There is likely to be almost as much variety within genders as there is between genders. Nonetheless, it helps to be aware of these tendencies in order to be a better listener and respond more effectively when people with different styles tell their stories.

Men tend to tell stories that preserve and enhance their sense of self-esteem and social status in relation to others. They identify themselves as independent problem-solvers and advisers, and their stories reflect this, often being concerned with their abilities and personal accomplishments. Sometimes this leads to stories seemingly being told to impress the listener; however, for a medical patient experiencing a severe threat to his sense of himself, such stories are less about self-aggrandizement than reassurance, an indirect attempt to deal with the uncertainty and self-doubt the storyteller may feel in his situation. The life narrative interview provides a useful framework for this communication style because the interviewer can easily focus on affirming the storyteller's sense of competence and accomplishment. The life challenges interview can further identify and emphasize the resources the individual can bring to bear on his current medical situation.

Women also tend to tell stories that preserve and enhance their sense of who they are, but their stories emphasize relationships and personal experiences that help them feel connected to the people in their lives. Rather than the instrumental, autonomous identity sought by men, women's identity is more often based on intimate relationships (Gilligan, 1982; MacCrae, 1990). For instance, a woman's a story about overcoming a difficulty is less likely to focus on the ingenuity of the solution to the problem than on the interactions and relationships that played a role in dealing with it. Women also tell stories with a goal of finding understanding and empathy from the listener, and it is obviously important for interviewers to be sensitive to such goals in severely ill medical patients. Interviewers can help a storyteller with this style to feel supported and understood through frequent empathic comments and some limited personal disclosure (see Chapter 6).

Although we have seen numerous examples of life narrative interviews that had gender-specific content and style, we could also list examples that confounded expectations. In addition, in an unpublished qualitative research project analyzing brief written accounts of life-changing experiences, we found that the ability of the two men and two women researchers (and an independent feminist narrative analyst) to identify the gender of the writers on the basis of themes and narrative styles was no better than chance. So while gender-specific styles and themes undoubtedly exist, making assumptions in advance about what specific storytellers will say or how they will say it is likely to be counterproductive. It remains important to be sensitive to individual storytellers and their narrative themes and styles.

With this in mind, another consideration is for the interviewer to become aware of his or her own gender-associated biases as a listener so that unconscious and unproductive patterns of questions and responses can be changed. A listener will have difficulty maintaining rapport with a significant proportion of patients if he or she asks questions only about how problems were solved as opposed to empathically reflecting the experience of the storyteller. Similarly, a listener who focuses only on the storyteller's emotional experiences and relationships, as opposed to what those experiences meant or what the storyteller accomplished, will leave many storytellers feeling unsettled and unsatisfied.

SHOULD INTERVIEWS WITH MINORITIES BE DIFFERENT?

Again, the answer here is yes and no. The process of the interview should be the same, but the interviewer should be alert to somewhat different themes that may emerge in the life story. This is particularly true for a life challenges interview. Although we have not done research in this area, we would not be surprised to find that the positive effects of life challenge interviews are more pronounced when the interview is conducted by an ethnic peer of the interviewee. Other researchers have found that interviewers with the same minority background are likely to get more richly detailed, more personal stories than interviewers from a different group, probably because of greater trust or the expectation that the interviewer is better able to understand the patient's experience (Yow, 1994).

Many members of minority groups have had negative experiences in their interactions with the majority culture or with other minorities. Examples of racism, bigotry, prejudice, discrimination, discouragement, and lost opportunities are a common part of the life experience of many minority groups. Perhaps even more than with gender, however, there are likely to be more varieties of experience within minority groups than between groups. Racism may have played a relatively small role for some people and may have been the defining experience for others. Again, being sensitive to the patient's own story is the most important goal for the interviewer.

Interestingly, our experience interviewing minority group members is that they often derive a great deal of self-esteem from their experiences in overcoming the many obstacles they have faced in trying to participate in the majority culture. Quite a few participants have been enthusiastic about discussing these topics. As always, the interviewer should test the waters with open-ended questions at first. After that, if these

TABLE 8.1   Life Challenges: Additional Questions for Minority Groups

Was it difficult preserving your cultural identity in the midst of the majority culture?

How important was your music, food, and religion for preserving your cultural identity?

Did you face much discrimination, bigotry, or racism? On the job? In your neighborhood? When you traveled? How did you handle it?

Did you and your family migrate from the south in search of a better life? What was that transition like for you? [For African-Americans who migrated from the south to the north]

Was it difficult making the transition from your native country? [For immigrants]

What forms of "culture shock" did you face? How did you manage to adjust?

Did you return to your original country to visit?

How did it feel to be a part of two different worlds?

issues appear relevant and can be discussed while maintaining the positive focus of the interview, interviewers might explore these areas with some of the supplemental challenge questions that we have found to be useful with minority groups (see Table 8.1).

As with gender issues, it is important for interviewers to examine their own experiences with minority groups to better understand and anticipate their own reactions to minority patients. These reactions may not be congruent with the patients' experience of themselves and may unconsciously result in unproductive questions or a loss of rapport. For instance, we assume that few of those in the majority American culture who read this book will have a conscious negative bias against African-American or Hispanic patients. Perhaps more of us may be inclined to respond to such patients as if they have fewer personal, social, and financial resources than they actually have, or as if an important part of their identity is that of a victim of racism. Such assumptions can subtly affect the rapport between the interviewer and patient.

Perhaps the best guideline across the board in interviewing anyone is: don't assume anything. The people you think are just like you probably aren't, and the people you think are different may have more in common with you than you suppose. Whether there is a difference or similarity in age, gender, or race, the assumptions that interviewers make based solely on a patient's membership in a social category need to be held lightly so that the interview can focus on the patient's unique experiences.

ARE THESE INTERVIEWS APPROPRIATE FOR PATIENTS WITH A TERMINAL ILLNESS?

Absolutely. As is the case with gender, race, and ethnic subgroups, terminally ill patients have more similarities than differences when compared with typical medical patients. Unfortunately, caregivers often view issues of death and dying as so paramount that other psychological issues are overlooked. Terminally ill patients have the same psychological needs as other patients and still have to cope with the usual variety of stressors, such as pain, physical limitations, side effects from treatment, and even boredom. Hence patients with terminal illness can benefit from life narrative interviews for the same reasons as other patients. In fact, hospice care programs are an ideal setting for conducting extended life narrative interviews.

However, medical caregivers also frequently make the mistake of not providing opportunities for patients to complete the "work of dying." In the hospital setting, where the mission is always to help patients get better, staff members sometimes have difficulty acknowledging the unique issues of the dying patient. For many individuals, an important task is to be able to tell the final version of their life story. Since others will be left to tell their story when they are gone, helping friends and family "get it right" can be an important objective for terminally ill patients.

Some health professionals may be concerned that by asking terminally ill patients to talk about their past lives, we might be sending an implicit negative message that there is no hope in their situation. We agree that maintaining a sense of hope is important for all patients who are in the late stages of a terminal illness. However, we have also found that these patients can usually work on the psychological tasks that accompany dying while still holding onto some hope that they will survive. For this reason, we would also strongly recommend that the health care provider never openly acknowledge the limited odds for survival unless the patient has taken the lead.

A brief description of the case of a 74-year-old Hispanic woman with end-stage metastatic breast cancer illustrates how life narrative interviews can be modified and used as part of an overall psychosocial intervention for this type of patient.

Mrs. Ramirez's primary care physician consulted a psychologist to help the patient cope with the severe pain from bone metastases and anxiety about a current lack of purpose in her life. She had coped well throughout the prior 15 years of her cancer, and had been open and courageous about the likelihood that the cancer would eventually take her life. Recently, however, her emotions took a turn for the worse as she lost her ability to do things for herself or others. She had viewed her primary role in life as a helper to others. She had always served as the emotional anchor of her very large family and could not tolerate being so needy. The final blow came when her husband was forced to retire from his job as a plumber to be a full-time caregiver.

The psychologist began his brief intervention by validating the patient's feeling that she had very little time left and that it seemed there were few useful things she could still do. After that, he conducted a 45-minute life narrative interview. It became clear that she had lived an impressive life, filled with many challenges successfully met. She told several inspiring stories: about her grandmother raising her in a rural Texas town; how she had to work doing laundry starting at age 12 to help support the family; how her first husband had been killed in World War II, leaving her with a newborn daughter; how she moved to Chicago and immediately met her husband of 48 years by chance at the train station; how she and her husband tried for 8 years before they could conceive a child; and how that son was ill throughout his childhood but eventually became very healthy, even athletic. The psychologist drew a connection between these events and her successful coping with cancer.

Fragments of these stories had been shared in the past, but the psychologist pointed out that there were too many important stories to be left to the chance recall of family and friends after she was gone. Also, since the patient worried that her family would be "lost" when she was no longer around, the psychologist helped her see how a permanent record of these positive stories would serve as guideposts for them when she was gone. She could easily relate to how the positive stories that her grandmother told had influenced her throughout her life. At the suggestion of the psychologist, the patient's husband and daughter agreed to conduct a series of videotaped interviews with the patient to record her life stories. Much of the information in this book was provided to the family as a guideline for their interviews.

The interviews were spread out over several weeks. The patient became increasingly animated as she went along and kept returning to earlier stories to add more details. As the process unfolded, the patient's pain gradually faded from being the focal point of her life to being only an annoying distraction. She died several months later, with her family reporting that she was at peace in her final days. The father and daughter made copies of the videotape and distributed them to other family members as a memorial gift.

HOW SHOULD CONFIDENTIALITY BE HANDLED?

Whenever someone tells us personal information in a professional context, it is important to think through the issues related to confidentiality.
Although life narrative interviews are not designed to probe particularly
sensitive material, patients are still more likely to share meaningful parts
of themselves in the interview if they know that the information they
share will remain confidential and not become a subject of gossip among
the hospital staff. It is therefore important for them to know who will learn
about the content of the interview and hear the audiotape. In most cases,
this would be restricted to the interviewer, peers in a supervision group,
and the program coordinator.

The patient may have some concerns about this that are difficult to
anticipate. One patient, for instance, had second thoughts after the interview was completed and was concerned that his family not hear about
his past. It is important to make clear to the patients that anyone they
do *not* want to hear the interview will not hear it.

In addition, where you intend a special use for the interview (e.g., as
a training tape), make sure the patient consents. We have been able to
include interview excerpts in this book because patients authorized their
interviews to be used for research and educational purposes as long as
they remained anonymous. It is also important to note that some hospitals have very specific rules about recording their patients and require
them to sign a consent form identifying the purpose of the recording.
Signing such a consent form can become the focal point for a broader
discussion of confidentiality with the patient.

HOW DO YOU EVALUATE THE EFFECTIVENESS
OF LIFE NARRATIVE INTERVIEWS?

Adding a way to confirm the value of life narrative interviews is optional,
but may be of value in a variety of ways. As with any new initiative within
the medical setting, administrators and scientifically minded staff members
will need to be convinced of the value of the program. You may also want
to assure yourself that the interviews are having a demonstrable positive
effect on patients. Although research has found results that justify this type
of program, there is always the possibility that the same findings would not
be replicated in a different medical setting with different participants.

When evaluation is a routine part of a life narrative interview program, it should use standardized, objective questionnaires. Standardized assessment enhances the likelihood of reliable findings and allows the project coordinator to communicate with the hospital administration and the scientific community (i.e., in a journal article or conference presentation) regarding outcomes of the project. If you decide to collect data on the outcomes of your interview program, we (the authors) would be pleased to hear from you about what you find.

We have found it useful to think of and measure outcomes of the interview on four different levels: (1) immediate psychological benefits following the interview; (2) coping benefits during the stressful medical event (i.e., a few hours later or a day later); (3) medical benefits during and after the stressful event; and (4) improved satisfaction with the hospital care received. Depending on your priorities, you may want to focus on only a few of these outcomes to reduce the paperwork burden on the patient.

The first area to evaluate is the extent to which the interview had the desired immediate effect on the patient's thoughts and feelings. The patient's anxiety before and after the interview can be measured with an abbreviated version of the State-Trait Anxiety Inventory (Spielberger, Gorsuch, & Lushene, 1970). An additional possibility to consider administering after the interview is the Coping Self-Efficacy Inventory (Rybarczyk & Auerbach, 1990; see Appendix A). This inventory measures the degree to which a participant has increased awareness of positive coping attributes.

The second area, coping during the procedure, can be assessed by measuring anxiety during the medical procedure or by assessing coping with a questionnaire designed for patients in that particular situation. For example, in our study involving coronary angioplasty, we assessed coping during the procedure with a questionnaire assessing the frequency of the most common positive and negative thoughts patients have during this procedure (Kendall et al., 1979: see Chapter 3).

The third area to evaluate, medical benefits, requires a more sophisticated and time-consuming data collection system and may not be possible in unfunded programs. The types of data that could be collected in this area include immunological functioning; the number of days until discharge after the stressful medical procedure; and the number of medications requested by and given to the patient to relieve pain, sleeplessness, and anxiety.

The final area of assessment is the patient's satisfaction with the intervention and the effect of the intervention on overall satisfaction with hospital care. These two areas can be measured with direct questions (e.g., "How satisfied were you with the life experience interview?" "How satisfied were you with the overall hospital care you received?") rated on a

1-to-5 Likert scale (ranging from "very dissatisfied" to "very satisfied"). Favorable findings in this outcome area alone can make the difference in obtaining support for the program from the hospital administration.

Probably the most important thing to keep track of, however, even if informally, is the enjoyment experienced by those who conduct the interviews. This is particularly true when volunteers are conducting the interviews, as described in Chapter 9. We are convinced that patients can benefit from the interview, but whether or not they are interviewed at all depends on how meaningful and enjoyable the people giving the interview find it. If the process of documenting and evaluating outcomes is burdensome to the point of jeopardizing the interviews themselves, our priorities are clear: cut back on evaluation and do the interviews. The benefits in terms of positive responses by patients to the interview and the resulting sense of satisfaction by the interviewers will be obvious to everyone involved.

REFERENCES

Borden, W. (1992). Narrative perspectives in psychosocial intervention following adverse life events. *Social Work, 37,* 135–141.

Brody, E. M. (1985). *Mental and physical health practices of older people.* New York: Springer.

Gilligan, C. (1982). *In a different voice: Psychological theory and women's development.* Cambridge, MA: Harvard University Press.

Gray, J. (1992). *Men are from Mars, women are from Venus.* New York: Harper-Collins.

Haight, B. K. (1991). Reminiscing: The State of the art as a basis for practice. *International Journal of Aging and Human Development, 33,* 1–32.

Kendall, P. C., Williams, L., Pechacek, T. F., Graham, L. E., Shisslak, C., & Herzoff, N. (1979). Cognitive-behavioral and patient education interventions in cardiac catheterization procedures: The Palo Alto medical psychology project. *Journal of Consulting and Clinical Psychology, 47,* 49–58.

Laird, J. (1989). Women and stories: Restorying women's self-constructing. In M. McGoldrick, C. Anderson, & F. Walsh (Eds.), *Women in families* (p. 448). New York: Norton.

MacCrae, H. (1990). Older women and identity maintenance in later life. *Canadian Journal on Aging, 9,* 248–267.

Merriam, S. B., & Cross, L. (1982). Adulthood and reminiscence: A descriptive study. *Educational Gerontology, 8,* 275–290.

Rybarczyk, B. D. & Auerbach, S. M. (1990). Reminiscence interviews as stress management interventions for older patients undergoing surgery. *The Gerontologist, 30,* 522–528.

Spielberger, C. D., Gorsuch, R., & Lushene, R. L. (1970). *Manual for the state anxiety inventory.* Palo Alto, CA: Consulting Psychologist Press.

Tannen, D. (1990). *You just don't understand: women and men in conversation.* New York: Ballantine.

Webster, J. D. (1995). Adult age differences in reminiscence functions. In B. K. Haight & J. D. Webster (Eds.), *The art and science of reminiscing: Theory, research, methods, and applications* (pp. 89–102). Washington, DC: Taylor & Francis.

Yow, V. R. (1994). *Recording oral history: a practical guide for social scientists.* Thousand Oaks, CA: Sage

CHAPTER 9

Setting Up a Volunteer Program for Life Narrative Interviews

*When you help someone up a hill,
you are a little nearer the top yourself.—Anonymous*

By now, we hope we have made the point that life narrative interviews conducted by medical professionals will yield substantial benefits to patients. However, given our experience that medical professionals are unlikely to be able to devote the time necessary to do a complete interview with all the patients who could benefit from one, developing alternative resources to conduct the interviews may be helpful.

A hospital program for life narrative interviews that uses volunteers is a "win-win-win" arrangement in which all parties benefit at no appreciable cost. The patient benefits from the enhancement to coping provided by the interview; the hospital benefits from increased satisfaction on the part of the interviewee, which is achieved without adding to the cost of care; and the volunteer benefits from the enrichment of participating in this type of project. In fact, these benefits may be favorable enough to attract funding for the program from a community or national funding agency.

ADVANTAGES OF USING VOLUNTEERS

Most hospitals have a volunteer service or an informal volunteer program. Not enough can be said about the generous individuals who give their time to work with people going through difficult experiences. Many volunteers are gifted and talented. They include retirees who have had successful careers in a wide variety of fields; there are also a great many younger adults and students who wish to give something back to the community. Although older volunteers typically have more time and energy to put into the program, we believe that a person from any age group can become an effective life narrative interviewer.

Many volunteers want to interact with and provide support to patients, but currently there are few opportunities to do so in most hospitals. Typically, volunteers perform such activities as delivering newspapers, mail, and flowers and providing religious support. These jobs are important and often place a volunteer in the position of providing informal emotional support. However, such tasks are not much of a challenge for individuals who have the desire and the natural skills to interact in a structured therapeutic way with patients and who lack only the training and opportunity to put their abilities to work.

Numerous studies have shown that properly trained and supervised peer counselors can be as effective as professionals when working with individuals who do not have actual psychopathologies—people who are "worried but well" (Durlak, 1979). Specifically, peer counselors have been effective in helping others adjust to such stressors as placement in a nursing home (Scharlach, 1988), retirement (Poser & Engels, 1983; Romaniuk & Priddy, 1980), and widowhood (Silverman, 1974). Peer helpers, as "similar others," are often better able to validate the experiences of the person who needs help, and better able to express empathic understanding (Thoits, 1986). Thus a volunteer may be particularly effective at life narrative interviews when he or she is an age-peer of the patient, because patient and interviewer are likely to share some similar life experiences.

In our first study, as mentioned, we compared older adult volunteers with younger graduate students who were training to be psychologists and found that the volunteers were equally effective (Rybarczyk & Auerbach, 1990). In both of our studies, we found that the volunteers were very enthusiastic about what they learned, the extent to which they were challenged, and the degree to which they felt they were providing an important service. They greatly valued individualized feedback regarding their strengths and the skills that needed improvement. Following the second study, the Chief of Staff and the Volunteer Services Department at Rush-Presbyterian-St. Luke's Medical Center presented our program with an award for using volunteers creatively and effectively. The award was given, in part, in recognition of the overwhelming enthusiasm among the volunteers involved in the project.

In addition, we have found that some hospital employees who have limited direct contact with patients are also interested in volunteering for this type of project. Their training and patient interviews can be arranged around their work schedule or after their work hours. These employees as volunteers have the additional advantage of already knowing the ins and outs of the medical center.

FINDING A COORDINATOR

The first task of setting up a volunteer program for life narrative is to designate a hospital staff member who will function as the program coordinator. This may or may not be the same person who has the idea for the program or lobbies the hospital administration to commit the few resources necessary to carry it through. The staff person who would serve best as the coordinator for the intervention program will vary from hospital to hospital. Certainly, any health professional on the hospital staff—such as a chaplain, social worker, nurse, recreational therapist, psychologist, or director of volunteer services—would be a candidate, depending on the responsibilities of his or her position. The initial role of the coordinator will be to determine the group of patients who will be offered the intervention, to gain the cooperation of other staff members who have those patients on their service or floor, and to establish a system for offering the intervention to the designated patients.

The coordinator may also be the person who recruits the patient for an interview (see the section on recruitment later in this chapter). Once a time for the interview is agreed upon, the coordinator calls volunteers to see who is available in that time slot. When an available volunteer is located, he or she is given the patient's name and room number. Because the number of patients who are interested in participating in the interview is not predictable, a group of volunteers need to be on call for any given day and time slot. The coordinator should attempt to rotate who gets the first phone call, the second, and so forth, so that each volunteer ends up having about the same number of opportunities to do an interview.

RECRUITING VOLUNTEER INTERVIEWERS

The second step in implementing a volunteer program is to develop a procedure to recruit, train, and supervise the volunteers. Recruitment of volunteers should begin with the volunteer services department at the hospital. Additional volunteers can be recruited from the community in order to obtain the largest possible group of individuals who have strong interpersonal skills and are motivated to become peer counselors. This may involve writing to the various volunteer or human service agencies in the community (e.g., United Way, AARP, RSVP, Volunteer Service Corps) and placing ads in newspapers and newsletters. A source of younger volunteers would be undergraduate universities and colleges where students are majoring in psychology, premed, or nursing. Notices in newsletters for religious congregations and other organizations whose membership includes a large number of retired persons are also a good bet. The recruitment notice should include a brief description of the project along with a reference to the personal benefits derived from participation (helping others, being challenged, and learning listening skills). It is important to keep in mind that this is an interesting opportunity for volunteers, and a strong response from the community can be expected.

Volunteers need not have any previous counseling experience or any particular level of education. Some of the best interviewers have been individuals without much education and individuals who have never held a paying job. They do need to commit themselves to completing the training and trying at least a couple of interviews to see if the process suits them. Another prerequisite is feeling comfortable with having their interviews audiotaped and evaluated by their peers or professional supervisors.

Persons who express an interest in volunteering should be carefully screened in a face-to-face interview before time is invested in their training. This is particularly true for volunteers who will administer the life challenges interview, which requires more skill. We found that the qualities that seem to predict who will be a successful interviewer include warmth, sensitivity, enthusiasm for getting to know others, and, of course, good listening skills. Volunteers who are garrulous or tend to be too nurturing when discussing emotional issues often have a difficult time conducting these interviews.

TRAINING AND SUPERVISING VOLUNTEERS

As we conducted our research studies, we found that it worked best to divide the training of the volunteers into two parts. The first part was the initial classroom instruction and practice interviews. Once the volunteer began conducting actual interviews, the second part of the training focused on supervision and feedback following each interview. In other words, we felt that it was important to view training as an ongoing process. This was conveyed to the volunteers by emphasizing that they should continually strive to improve their performance. For hospital volunteers who are not involved in a research project, supervision time can be reduced once they have achieved an adequate level of competence in actual interviews.

The first part of the training includes training classes and practice interviews. Two 3-hour classes are adequate to provide an introduction to the whys and hows of the life experience interview. It helps to restrict the class to about four to six members. This allows each volunteer to receive individualized instruction and to establish relationships with the coordinator and the other class members. Investing time and energy in a high-quality class experience for the volunteers pays dividends in fostering motivation and improving results.

The agenda for the two classes follows the general outline used for this book. The first class provides an introduction to the general concept of the life narrative interview, a rationale for using it as a stress intervention, and the basics on how to administer it (e.g., techniques for starting, guiding, and ending the interview). The second class covers the finer points of conducting a general life experience interview (LEI), a review of questions to ask; and, for those learning the life challenges interview (LCI), a section on how to add the "challenge" items to the interview. At the end of the class, difficult situations can be addressed that might be encountered during an interview (e.g., interruptions and sad memories).

We recommend that each of the two classes feature a demonstration videotape of a successful interview, audiotapes of interviews by other volunteers, class members pairing up to role-play different situations in an interview, and homework involving reading the list of interview questions and several nonacademic articles about reminiscence. The coordinator may wish to produce demonstration audiotapes or videotapes before proceeding with the program. As noted in chapter 8, the patient's consent should be obtained when a tape is used for training. The readings can be mailed to volunteers in advance of the classes. Several useful articles may be obtained from the AARP training guide on conducting reminiscence group therapy (AARP, 1989). The book you are now reading would also serve as a good companion to classroom instruction.

In designing training classes for older adult volunteers, several principles should be applied to maximize learning. First, the pace of learning needs to be slower. Second, learning should closely follow a progression from basic skills to more complex skills. Third, classes should incorporate as many active learning techniques as possible, such as frequent question-and-answer periods and role-playing. Fourth, the requisite skills should be modeled wherever possible in demonstrations, or on video- or audiotape. Finally, the instruction must include ongoing and immediate feedback regarding progress.

Following the two introductory classes, the coordinator can arrange for each volunteer to conduct a practice interview with a patient who is not facing a stressful medical event (e.g., someone admitted for a routine procedure). The interview may be audiotaped and then carefully reviewed with the volunteer. An interview checklist has been developed to serve as a guideline for providing feedback to the interviewer (see Appendix D). When necessary, additional practice sessions can be arranged until the volunteer is able to meet the criterion for skill. This criterion is not mastery of the interview but rather the ability to achieve the basic process goals and demonstration of an adequate level of active listening (see Chapters 4 and 6). Volunteers are not used in the program until they have reached this level.

About one third of our volunteers have been able to meet the criterion on the first try and another third after a second practice session. But some volunteers need several practice sessions, and some volunteers are never able to get the hang of it. This last group can be politely referred to another volunteer activity that would better suit their strengths.

Extra practice sessions may be needed in many cases for additional work on listening skills. Becoming a good listener is sometimes a formidable challenge for volunteers who are accustomed to participating in two-way conversations. Volunteers who fall into this category can be given remedial training in the form of listening exercises. A good exercise commonly used by marriage counselors to improve communication is to have one person listen to another talking about a subject for 5 minutes without interruption. After the time has expired, the listener is then asked to review the information that was conveyed. The original speaker then follows up by pointing out details that were left out. Speaker and listener then reverse roles. When repeated several times, this drill results in significant improvements and an increased awareness of what it takes to be a good listener.

Another important part of the training is the ongoing supervision and feedback provided by the coordinator. The supervision sessions (often conducted by telephone) that follow the first few interviews serve several functions. First, they give the interviewers an outlet for sharing feelings and ideas generated by the interview. This often includes a good deal of enthusiasm as well as new insights into how interviews could be improved. Second, having the coordinator review the tapes ensures quality control by allowing for immediate feedback when an interviewer veers off track. Finally, as interviewers progress, the feedback can be tailored more and more toward fine-tuning their skills.

A peer supervision group would reduce time demands on the coordinator and may even serve an important training function by encouraging interviewers to see themselves as emerging experts. The interviewers could convene each week to listen to each other's interview tapes from the previous week, provide encouragement and feedback, and share feelings about their interviewing experiences. The coordinator would serve as the moderator of the group. Like the "quality circles" used in business settings, this group could also provide a forum for discussing improvements that can be made in the logistics of the volunteer program.

RECRUITING PATIENTS
TO PARTICIPATE IN THE PROGRAM

People do not always know what they like until they try it. Because life narrative interviews are designed to be administered to persons who are in the midst of a stressful event and are probably anxious, many patients will at first be hesitant about participating when the interview is offered. Although many individuals can detect immediately that you are offering something for their benefit and will become enthusiastic about participating in the interview, some will require a bit of persuasion. In our own research projects, coordinators were able to average a surprisingly high consent rate: 70% of the patients who were invited to participate. Participation in an interview program that is not part of a research project is likely to be even higher, since there are no questionnaires to be filled out.

Depending on the setting and the resources available, different people may be involved in recruiting patients to be interviewed by volunteers. It is probably best to have an employee with some authority (e.g., a nurse, a social worker, a psychologist) serve as the recruiter, as opposed to a volunteer. Once the life narrative interview program has established a reputation for providing a valuable service to patients, other staff members may become interested in recruiting patients. In-service presentations to other staff members will also promote awareness of the program. Using a staff person to recruit patients lends more initial credibility to the interview and probably increases the chance that the patient will participate. But it seems best not to leave the recruitment to busy people who have no particular investment in the program.

If it is not possible to use an employee, a volunteer can recruit patients. The volunteer should mention that the interview is endorsed by the hospital administration as well as by the patient's attending physician.

Whoever offers the interview to the patient must be enthusiastic about the value of the interview. At the very least, the recruiter should be able to say confidently that the experience is almost always enjoyable for participants, since the confidence of the initial contact person is critical to the patient's willingness to participate. In our two studies, confidence and lack of confidence appeared to account for much of the variability in the success rates of different recruiters.

It also helps to practice the introduction to the interview before using it with patients. The following is an example of an introduction to the interview that was used in a study with coronary angioplasty patients.

I: *Good afternoon, my name is Barbara Willis. I work with the Life Experience Interview Program here at the hospital. We invite patients who are undergoing medical procedures to participate in an interview that asks them to share stories about their positive life experiences. This interview would take place tomorrow during the waiting period before your procedure. The purpose is to create an enjoyable experience for both you and the interviewer, who is a trained volunteer, and to get you in a positive frame of mind before your procedure. From our experience with other patients, we've found that the interview can help things go more smoothly.*

If the patient agrees to participate, the recruiter then asks if he or she would have any objection to being audiotaped. At this point, the policy on confidentiality should be explained. The recruiter should also explain that the purpose of taping is to provide a means for coaching interviewers on how they can improve. We found that almost all participants were agreeable to being audiotaped. In fact, many participants seemed both flattered and motivated by the fact that we considered the interview important enough to tape.

The timing of recruitment of patients is also important. Although an interview can be conducted immediately after it has been proposed, this may be disruptive to the patient's coping strategies if he or she is expecting to undergo a medical treatment of some type later that day. In our two studies, patients were recruited either the day before or several hours before the actual interview. If surgical patients are included in the program, experience suggests that it is best to ask them shortly after they enter the hospital and get settled into their rooms. In the current state of hospital economics, surgical patients are often admitted the evening before or the day of their surgery. If surgery is scheduled for very early in the morning, a life narrative interview can be conducted the night before.

When medical procedures are scheduled well in advance and you have the cooperation of the physician (and when there's time), a brief letter can be sent beforehand describing the interview and informing patients that they will be contacted after being admitted. The letter should include a rationale for the interview and perhaps some quotations from satisfied former participants. Here's an excerpt from a letter one coronary angioplasty patient (P) wrote to us after participating in an interview.

> P: The interview was a wonderful way to take my mind off the operation that was coming up that afternoon. It made me feel so much better to sit and talk to someone about things that brought back so many memories—some things that even my family members had never heard about! It was a lot better way to spend the time before an operation than having someone sitting there, saying "you're going to be fine," when I was so worried. Doing the interview was a first in my life and certainly was a terrific experience!

EVALUATING THE EFFECTIVENESS OF THE VOLUNTEER PROGRAM

In addition to the four outcomes for patients covered in Chapter 8 (immediate psychological benefits, coping benefits during the procedure, medical benefits, and increased satisfaction), the impact that conducting the interviews has on the volunteers can be evaluated as well. This can provide information on what types of individuals are well suited to the program and how their satisfaction compares with that of volunteers who participate in other hospital programs. A Volunteer Satisfaction Questionnaire that we developed and used for our most recent study is included in Appendix E. A questionnaire can also be used to solicit feedback from the volunteers on improving logistical matters, such as supervision and case assignment.

As we've already noted, the skills required to listen to patients' stories are well suited to the talents of many volunteers, and the contact with patients is likely to be highly satisfying for them. The life narrative interview can easily become one of the mainstays of a hospital volunteer program and one of the most sought-after volunteer activities. We see it as a way not only to enhance the patient's hospital experience but also to provide an incentive for talented people to volunteer and a solid building block for a hospital volunteer program.

REFERENCES

American Association of Retired Persons. (1989). *Reminiscence: Finding meaning in memories. Training guide.* Washington, DC: Author.

Durlak, J. A. (1979). Comparative effectiveness of paraprofessionals and professional helpers. *Psychological Bulletin, 86,* 80–92.

Poser, E. G., & Engels, M. L. (1983). Self-efficacy assessment and peer group assistance in a preretirement intervention. *Educational Gerontology, 9,* 159–169.

Romaniuk, M., & Priddy, J. (1980). Widowhood and peer counseling. *Counseling and Values, 24,* 195–203.

Rybarczyk, B. D., & Auerbach, S. M. (1990). Reminiscence interviews as stress management interventions for older patients undergoing surgery. *The Gerontologist, 30,* 522–528.

Scharlach, A. E. (1988). Peer counseling training for nursing home residents. *The Gerontologist, 28,* 499–502.

Silverman, P. (1974). *Helping each other in widowhood.* New York: Health Sciences Press.

Thoits, P. A. (1986). Social support as coping assistance. *Journal of Consulting and Clinical Psychology, 54,* 416–423.

CHAPTER 10

Afterword:
Why We Need Our Stories

A story has power over life. The act of telling a story or listening to it is a taking in of the story's power.—Jane Yolen

As we've seen, stories are ways of looking at the world. Our stories orient us to our circumstances and tell us who we are, what we can and can't do, whether the world is safe or unsafe, what's right and wrong, and what's important and not important. As we said in Chapter 1, stories define meaning, identity, and relationships in the context of our lives and help us make sense of what is going on. In the form of the life narrative interview, stories reduce anxiety and uncertainty by helping us remember and feel accepted for who we are and the resources we have.

But do we really *need* our stories in the same way we might need, say, chemotherapy for cancer? In the context of a medical problem and medical care, do patients need their stories? We think they do. When patients are noncompliant or refuse treatment, when they seek out second opinions or alternative treatments, when they insist on hearing about options for treatment and making their own choices, we are witnessing their need for their own story. This is most obvious to us at times when the patient's story differs from the biomedical agenda and we can therefore see it more clearly. But a patient's story is equally important and powerful when it is relatively invisible in the medical context—when the patient uses it to ally himself or herself with medical caregivers and treatment.

119

The life narrative interviews described in this book are a method for building that alliance with patients. In realizing (perhaps somewhat to their surprise) that their own life stories have a place in the medical context, patients can relax and feel accepted. They are no longer identified (and they no longer identify themselves) primarily by their medical problems. They are Mr. Jones, the autoworker who built Ford Mustangs; and Ms. Smith, the lawyer who argued a case before the state supreme court. In identifying and supporting patients as individual human beings, the interview aligns the medical context with the patient's story. This reduces patients' anxiety and improves their ability to cope with their illnesses.

In a way, it is ironic that simply telling a story about the positive experiences of one's life is capable of making one more relaxed and better able to tolerate a medical illness and treatment. It speaks to the question of the source of patients' anxiety and maladaptive coping. Is all such distress intrinsic to having the disease itself? Clearly not, since much of it is subject to change with a simple intervention. Much of the anxiety and distress that patients experience during the course of an illness and even attribute to their illness is actually caused by the medical environment and the relationships patients have with caregivers. The anxiety and distress are often caused by the context we have created for the care of illness, not by the disease itself.

To the extent that this is true, it is a statement about how far the biomedical perspective and medical practices have drifted from a focus on patients' experience of their illnesses and from the comfort and reassurance that earlier medical practitioners offered when they had little else to give. Today, admission to the medical system largely means that patients have their stories taken away from them. When patients enter a hospital, their sense of themselves as comfortably competent is changed, like their clothing, into something that, from a psychological perspective, is cold, flimsy, and revealing and makes them feel vulnerable. In contrast, the life narrative approach is a way of bringing the patients' identity and internal resources into the foreground in a way that helps them to cope more effectively with their illness and promotes their well-being long into the future.

Finally, we want to emphasize how rewarding these interviews can be for the medical caregiver. Some of our most gratifying experiences with patients have been in the context of a life narrative interview. These feelings were well expressed by Dan McAdams (1993), who has conducted many similar interviews in the course of his pioneering research on the relationship of life stories to personal identity. Interestingly, he was not trying to be therapeutic in his interviews. He was taping the life stories of his subjects for research purposes.

> At the end of the interview, most people report that the experience of telling their stories was profoundly satisfying and enjoyable, even if they shed tears in the telling. . . . They hope dearly that they did not bore me. The truth is I am never bored, nor are my students. Instead we feel privileged to be given such a sincere self-disclosure—such a precious gift of intimacy. I feel my daily interactions are rarely as real and as authentic as the interviews I have on tape. (pp. 252–253)

We hope to see these interviews used creatively in a wide variety of medical situations. Tell us your story about using them. You can write to us:

Bruce Rybarczyk, Ph.D.
Department of Psychology
Rush-Presbyterian-St. Luke's Medical Center
1653 West Congress Parkway
Chicago, IL 60612

REFERENCES

McAdams, D. P. (1993). *The stories we live by.* New York: Morrow.
Yolen, J. (1991). *Best-loved stories told at the National Storytelling Festival.* Jonesborough, TN: National Storytelling Press.

Appendixes

APPENDIX A

Coping Self-Efficacy Inventory

DIRECTIONS: Circle the response that best describes how much you agree with each statement.

	Not at all true	Somewhat true	Moderately true	Very much true
1. I am a very determined person.	1	2	3	4
2. I handle fear better than the average person.	1	2	3	4
3. I become frustrated when I experience physical discomfort.	1	2	3	4
4. I can cope with the setbacks of life better than the average person.	1	2	3	4
5. I have the ability to "grin and bear it" when faced with a difficulty I can't change.	1	2	3	4
6. I handle stress very well.	1	2	3	4

Appendix B

Questions for the Life Experience Interview

Childhood Years

To emphasize the chronological ordering of the interview, it is helpful to begin by saying, "I'd like to start with your childhood years."

The Start

- What is your earliest childhood memory? (Many counselors consider this question the fastest way to get to the most important themes in a person's early life.)
- Where were you born?
- Who were you named after?
- What does your last name mean?
- Did you grow up in the country or city?
- Were you ever told any stories about your birth?
- How many brothers and sisters did you have?
- Where did you fit in the birth order?
- What were you like as a young child?
- What did you look like?

Home Life

- What was your childhood home like? Your bedroom? Describe it.
- Describe the neighborhood that you grew up in.
- Did you have a family pet that you remember fondly?
- Tell me about your first "best friend."

- What kinds of adventures did you have together? What kinds of games did you play together?
- Did your family sit down for dinner each evening? What was dinner like?
- What family recipes do you remember most?
- Did your family gather to listen to the radio or watch TV?
- What holidays or birthdays are memorable for you?
- What was the family routine on weekends? Sundays? Summer days?
- Did your family have a car?
- Was religion important to you and your family?

Parents and Other Adults

- What were your parents like when you were a child?
- What line of work was your father in? Did your mother work outside the home?
- Were your parents immigrants? What stories did they tell you about the "old country"?
- Other than your parents, was there an adult in your life with whom you had a close relationship? Someone you looked up to? Maybe an aunt, an uncle, or a teacher?
- Did your family ever travel a long distance to visit a relative? To attend family picnics or reunions?

Interests and Hobbies

- Do you remember what you fantasized about becoming when you grew up? Did you play games of make-believe?
- What games or toys did you like most as a child?
- What was daily life like around your house during your childhood?
- What stories captured your imagination as a child? What books? TV or radio programs? Movies? Comic books? Magazines?
- Who were your heroes or heroines in stories?
- Were you interested in cooking? Needlework? Sewing?
- Did you ever make a quilt or some other large piece of work?
- Did you collect anything? Baseball cards? Stamps? Coins? Shells?
- Did you have an interest in crafts or gardening?
- Did you play a musical instrument?
- Did you keep a diary? Did you keep it secret? How?
- Were you a fan of a sports team? Did you have a favorite player?
- Did you ever go to see a circus? A parade?

Rural Life

- What kind of farm did your family have?
- Did you have animals?
- What did you like about growing up in a farm community?
- What chores did you have to do?
- How early did you get up?
- What was your favorite season of the year? Why?

Urban Life

- What did you like about growing up in the city?
- Was yours an ethnic neighborhood? Was there a lot of flavor from the "old county" in your neighborhood?
- Did you travel by streetcar?
- Was there a corner store, a grocery, a meat market?
- Did your parents, family, and friends gather at a local tavern? Were children sometimes included?

TEENAGE YEARS

School

- How far did you get in school?
- How did you get to school each day?
- What were your favorite subjects in school? Why?
- Do you remember how you spent recess?
- What did you eat at lunchtime?
- Tell me about a class or teacher you remember most.
- What job did you aspire to as a teenager? What job did your parents want you to study for?
- Did you discover a talent for any type of art during your teen years?
- Were there sports you played that were important to you?

Friends

- Who did you hang around with as a teenager? Was it a tight group of friends?
- Did your group get into any mischief?
- What type of crowd was it?
- Where did you and your friends hang out?
- Did you and your friends have any favorite expressions or nicknames for each other?

Dating

- When did you first begin to notice that you felt sexually attracted to another person?
- Can you remember your first date?
- What clothes were in style when you started dating?
- What was considered "proper" dress at the time?
- Were you chaperoned?
- Did you like to dance? Did you like to go to dances?
- Can you remember taking your first date to the movies?
- Did you go to the prom? What did you wear?
- Tell me about the first time you "fell in love."

Adventures

- What kinds of dreams and ambitions did you have for your life?
- Did you have any unusually memorable summer vacations?
- What was the first car that you drove?
- How important to you was riding or driving around in cars?
- What was the first trip you took away from home?
- Do any train or plane rides stick in your memory?
- Did you go to any county or state fairs? Amusement parks? Beaches?

YOUNG ADULTHOOD

Marriage

- Are you married?
- How did you meet your spouse? How old were you?
- What was your courtship like?
- What did you have in common? What attracted you to each other?
- Describe your wedding.
- Where did you go for your honeymoon?
- Describe the first apartment you rented.
- Describe the first house you purchased.

College and First Job

- What was your first full-time job? Did you like it?
- What did it feel like to make "real" money for the first time?
- Did you go to college? How did you select it?

- What was college like for you? What's your favorite memory from college?
- Were you a member of a sorority or fraternity?
- Do you remember any college pranks?
- What traditions of your school were important to you?

Milestones

- What was the first car you owned?
- Did you live on your own before marriage?
- What was your first apartment like? Did you have roommates?
- What were your wartime experiences?
- Did you make good friends in the military?
- Did you get to see a lot of the world?

FAMILY AND CAREER YEARS

Raising a Family

- Do you have children? How many?
- What happy memories do you have of your kids when they were very young?
- What made them happy as kids?
- Can you remember some humorous things that happened with the kids?
- What were your happiest times with your kids?
- What was the most satisfying thing about being a parent?

Career

- What is (was) your career?
- How did you end up in that career?
- What was the most exciting point in your career?
- Did you have any mentors that influenced the direction of your career?

Key Events

- Did you ever attend any major national events? (e.g., the Olympics, a political convention)

- Did you attend a high school reunion? Which one sticks in your mind the most? What realizations did you have about how you had changed since high school?
- What is the most memorable vacation you took?

SUMMARY QUESTIONS

- What has been the most rewarding thing in your life so far?
- What have been the greatest blessings in your life?
- What things are you most thankful for in your life?

Appendix C

Questions for the Life Challenges Interview

Childhood Years

Home Life

- Were you raised in a large family? [If the answer is yes] That can be challenging. How did you make the best of it?
- Did you learn to share with siblings at a young age?
- When did you learn to be able to be alone and play by yourself? What special places did you have for being by yourself?
- What rules did your parents require you to follow?
- Did you benefit in some way from those rules?
- What creative things did your family do to beat the heat in the summer?
- Did you have any fears as a child that you now laugh at when you look back? How did you overcome them?
- Did your family have less than other families in the neighborhood?
- How did you learn to make do with less than kids have today?
- If your parents were immigrants, did they speak English at home?
- Did you have to struggle to balance the things your parents wanted you to retain from the "old country" with the ways of the "new country"?
- How did the Great Depression affect your family?
- What creative things did your family do to make ends meet?
- Did you or your family pitch in for the "war effort" in the early 1940s?
- Do you remember rationing? What sacrifices do you remember making? Did you raise, can, or preserve your own food?
- Did your family experience any unusual events (e.g., a fire, a tornado)? How did you and your family cope with these events?

133

- Did your family ever move when you were growing up? How did you make the adjustment?

Parents and Other Adults

- What positive values and ideals did your parents convey to you?
- What lessons did you learn from your parents?
- Did they work hard to get ahead?
- What teacher or other adult managed to inspire you to do your best?
- How did he or she inspire you?

Hobbies and Interests

- Do you remember learning to ride a bike? What was it like?
- Do you remember learning how to swim? Were you frightened at first?
- How did you manage to have fun without all the toys and games that kids have today? What creative things did you do?
- If your family had less time and money for recreation, did that make you appreciate the fun that was available even more?
- Were there any sports, games, or skills that you worked extra hard to be good at when you were a kid?
- Did you learn to play a musical instrument? Did it take a tremendous amount of practice to learn? How did you maintain the discipline that it took?

Rural Life

- What hard lessons did you learn about life while living on a farm?
- Did you have lots of chores to do each day? Which chore were you best at? Which chore did you like least? What did you do to make it as pleasant as possible?
- With less farm machinery back then, in what ways did you have to improvise to get things done?
- Do you remember having to work extra hard during a bad year?
- What was the work like during bad weather?
- What was it like trying to go to school and still having to do chores in the morning? Did that help you develop self-discipline?

Urban Life

- What did you learn from living in the city about getting along with other people?

- Were there any places you had to avoid to stay out of danger?
- Were there any "tough characters" in your neighborhood?

TEENAGE YEARS

School

- How did you discover your strengths and abilities early in life?
- Did you have a long walk to get to school each day?
- What was your best subject? What made you good at it?
- Was there a subject that you did not do well with at first but managed to excel at later?
- Did you have any special achievements or honors in school?

Friends

- How did you make friends during those awkward teenage years, when it is so easy to feel insecure?
- Did you have any challenges to cope with when relating to your peers, such as being shorter than average, not being athletic, or being from a family that was not wealthy? Did the challenges eventually become less important? Can you remember how you overcame them?
- Did you face peer pressure in matters such as interests, dress, dating, smoking, or drinking? How did you deal with it?

Dating

- Were you shy around girls or boys? How did you get past that?
- Was it difficult to ask a girl or boy out for a first date?
- Did you feel good about yourself when you realized that girls or boys were attracted to you?
- Did you struggle with your parents over dating?
- Did your parents allow you to wear makeup?
- Who was the first girlfriend or boyfriend to "break your heart"?
- Were you surprised to discover that you could get over it?

Adventures

- How did you learn to drive a car? Were there any obstacles to learning how to drive?
- Can you remember the first time you went away from home for an extended period of time? Did it take some time to adjust?

YOUNG ADULTHOOD

Marriage

- What challenges did you face in the early days of your marriage?
- How did you learn to work out your differences?

College and First Job

- Was your first full-time job hard work?
- How did you adjust to working full time?
- What did you have to go through to get the job?
- Were there other jobs that you were able to find that were hard to get? What strengths and resources did you use to get a job?
- What did you have to do to get into college?
- Did your parents help pay? Did you have to work while in school?
- Was it a difficult decision whether to raise a family or get further education? Were you able to do both?

Milestones

- Do you remember "leaving home" for good? How did it feel?
- Was that a turning point in your life?
- What did you have to go through to purchase your first home?
- What were your experiences during World War II? How did they make you a better or stronger person?
- Were you separated from your spouse during the war? What sort of challenges did that pose?
- Did you have to raise a family on your own while your spouse was in the service?
- What was boot camp like? Was it a long way from home?
- Were you scared when you went overseas?
- Were you afraid of dying in the war?
- What was difficult about the place where you were stationed?
- Did you meet people who inspired you during the war?
- How did they influence you toward personal growth?

FAMILY AND CAREER YEARS

Raising a Family

- What challenges did you face in pregnancy? In giving birth?
- What values did you strive to impart to your kids?

- What did you do to ensure that your kids grew up with the kinds of values you believe are important?
- What unexpected challenges did parenting bring? How did you get past them?
- How did being a parent make you a better or stronger person?

Career

- What were you really good at in your job?
- What problems did you handle effectively?
- Were there any career transitions that you had to make?
- Did you get promoted during your career? What qualities did you have that allowed you to get ahead in your job?
- Did you face any sexism in the workplace?
- What were the challenges of managing a home mostly on your own while your husband was busy with his career?
- What were the challenges of a dual-career marriage?

Key Events

- At your high school reunions, did you become aware of ways that you had changed for the better?
- Did you make a contribution to your neighborhood or church?
- Were you an officeholder in any organization?
- What obstacles did you have to work around to get this accomplished?
- Did you ever move your family from one community to another? What was it like to start all over again?

SUMMARY QUESTIONS

- What is the biggest challenge that you have faced in your life?
- What lessons has life taught you?
- If someone wrote a book about your life, what would he or she say is the most remarkable thing you have achieved?
- What was your proudest moment?
- What was your finest hour?
- What key events shaped your life?
- On the basis of your life experiences, what is your philosophy of life?

APPENDIX D

Interview Review Checklist

Items	Weaker point → Strength of interview				
1. Following basic guidelines:					
a. Elicited positive memories	1	2	3	4	5
b. Followed threads chronologically	1	2	3	4	5
c. Stayed with personal memories	1	2	3	4	5
d. Elicited seldom-accessed memories	1	2	3	4	5
e. Avoided negative memories	1	2	3	4	5
f. Storytelling was descriptive	1	2	3	4	5
g. Covered most of life cycle	1	2	3	4	5
2. Active listening:					
a. Concentrated at high level	1	2	3	4	5
b. Empathized when appropriate	1	2	3	4	5
c. Used silence effectively	1	2	3	4	5
d. Used summaries	1	2	3	4	5
e. Used process comments	1	2	3	4	5
3. Finer points:					
a. Questions elicited positive feelings	1	2	3	4	5
b. Kept interview on emotional level	1	2	3	4	5
c. Evoked reflective responses	1	2	3	4	5
d. Questions flowed from stories	1	2	3	4	5
e. Avoided present topics	1	2	3	4	5
4. Life challenges interview:					
a. Accomplished basic life narrative	1	2	3	4	5
b. Added focus on challenges	1	2	3	4	5
c. Underscored strengths and resources	1	2	3	4	5
d. Summarized key strengths and resources	1	2	3	4	5

Appendix E

Volunteers' Satisfaction Questionnaire

1. I feel very satisfied with the volunteer work that has been assigned to me.

Very much true		Moderately true		Not at all true
1	2	3	4	5

2. I have found pleasure and enjoyment in my volunteer work.

Very much true		Moderately true		Not at all true
1	2	3	4	5

3. I feel that I am an important part of the hospital.

Very much true		Moderately true		Not at all true
1	2	3	4	5

4. I feel that I have helped others through my volunteer work.

Very much true		Moderately true		Not at all true
1	2	3	4	5

5. My volunteer work has been personally fulfilling.

Very much true		Moderately true		Not at all true
1	2	3	4	5

6. My volunteer work has been challenging.

Very much true		Moderately true		Not at all true
1	2	3	4	5

7. I feel that my talents were utilized in my volunteer work.

Very much true		Moderately true		Not at all true
1	2	3	4	5

Index

℔ *Springer Publishing Company*

Aging and Biography
Explorations in Adult Development

James E. Birren, PhD, **Gary M. Kenyon,** PhD
Jan-Erik Ruth, PhD, **Johannes J.F. Schroots,** PhD
Torbjorn Svensson, PhD, Editors

Personal life narratives can serve as a rich source of new insights into the experience of human aging. In this comprehensive volume, an international team of editors and contributors provide effective approaches to using biography to enhance our understanding of adult development. Chapters include discussion of theories, methods, and applications of biographical techniques for examining middle-aged and older adults.

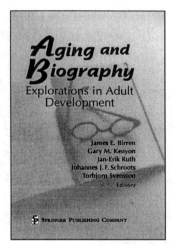

Partial Contents:
- Biography in Adult Development, *Jan-Erik Ruth and Gary Kenyon*
- The Meaning-Value of Personal Storytelling, *Gary M. Kenyon*
- Emotionality and Continuity in Biographical Contexts, *Wilhelm Mader*
- Studying Older Lives: Reciprocal Acts of Telling and Listening, *Bertram J. Cohler and Thomas R. Cole*
- Competence and Quality of Life: Continuity and Discontinuity in Autobiography, *Johannes J.F. Schroots*
- Narrating the Self in Adulthood, *Dan P. McAdams*
- The Complexity of Personal Narratives, *Brian de Vries and Allen J. Lehman*
- Biographical Assessment in Community Care, *Brian Gearing and Peter Coleman*
- Guided Autobiography: Exploring the Self and Encouraging Development, *James Birren and Betty Birren*

1995   368pp   0-8261-8980-6   *hardcover*

536 Broadway, New York, NY 10012-3955 • (212) 431-4370 • Fax (212) 941-7842

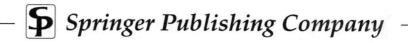 **Springer Publishing Company**

Reminiscence and the Self in Old Age
Edmund Sherman, PhD

"...timely, providing a perspective on the uses and functions of reminiscence by older persons...Sherman's is a book that will turn the afternoon of life into an unusual humanizing experience."

—from the Foreword by James E. Birren, PhD

"...[researchers] will find a wealth of information about the problems encountered in attempts to do research concerning reminiscence, just as clinicians will find...a great many useful suggestions to aid them in understanding elderly clients."

—Clinical Gerontologist

Contents:

- Forms and Functions of Reminiscence
- The Experience of Reminiscence
- The Language of Reminiscence
- The Aging Self
- Of Time and Objects
- Life Themes in Reminiscence
- Variations on a Theme
- The Art of Reminiscence
- Private Endings

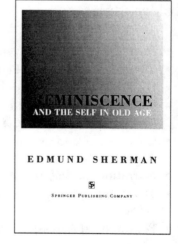

1991   288pp   0-8261-7550-3   hardcover

536 Broadway, New York, NY 10012-3955 • (212) 431-4370 • Fax (212) 941-7842

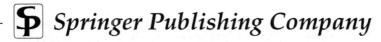
Springer Publishing Company

Interpreting the Aging Self
Personal Journals of Later Life

Harry J. Berman, PhD
Foreword: **Sheldon Tobin,** PhD

Through careful review of a fascinating collection of diaries, Dr. Berman explores what it is to be an older person. In this insightful, well-written volume the author weaves a conceptual background of three major themes: the emerging qualitative approach to psychological inquiry known as human science, the long tradition of studying personal documents in psychology, and the recent attempts to constitute a hermeneutic (interpretive/critical) gerontology.

The author focuses on five specific diarists, Elizabeth Vining, Doris Grumbach, Alan Olmstead, Florida Scott-Maxwell, and May Sarton, to examine how aging affects self-understanding and how the self is related to the writing of personal journals. He then concludes with a discussion of the implications of the study of older people's writings for our ideas about what constitutes knowledge of aging. The volume will appeal to both psychologists and gerontologists, as well as academics and researchers interested in personality and the self, lifespan development, and adulthood and aging.

Contents:

- Introduction
- Human Science and the Use of Personal Documents
- Diaries, Journals, and Personal Journals
- Elizabeth Vining and the Transition to Later Adulthood
- May Sarton and the Tensions of Attachment
- Doris Grumbach: Recovery from Despair
- Alan Olmstead and the Fashioning of Purpose
- Florida Scott-Maxwell: Individuation in the Face of Frailty
- Diaries, Narrative, and the Self
- What is "Knowledge of Aging" Knowledge of?

1994   248pp   0-8261-8060-4   hardcover

536 Broadway, New York, NY 10012-3955 • (212) 431-4370 • Fax (212) 941-7842

Springer Publishing Company

Increasing Patient Satisfaction
A Guide for Nurses

Roberta L. Messner, RNC, PhD, CPHQ
Susan J. Lewis, RN, PhD, CS

This manual guides nurses and others in the health care setting through the fundamentals of ensuring a satisfied "customer." It illustrates the many components of quality care, including how to provide clear and adequate information, create a hospitable environment, handle complaints efficiently, and design and utilize surveys of client satisfaction.

The authors draw from the principles of continuous quality improvement and other lessons learned from the business world, in addition to nursing's rich tradition of service. Written with warmth, sensitivity, and clarity, the book is an excellent resource for nursing students and practicing nurses. Health care institutions seeking good client relations will find this a suitable text for in-service training.

Contents:

What Do Patients Really Want? • The Changing American Healthcare Scene and Patient Satisfaction • Quality Isn't a Coincidence • Yes, Patients Do Have Rights • Patient Education: A Key to Increased Satisfaction • Creating a Hospitable and Healing Environment • How to Handle a Customer Complaint • Looking for the Lesson: Measuring/Evaluating Patient Satisfaction Findings • Be Kind to Yourself and Your Coworkers: A Plan for Enhanced Morale and Patient Satisfaction

1996   240pp   0-8261-9250-5   hardcover

536 Broadway, New York, NY 10012-3955 • (212) 431-4370 • Fax (212) 941-7842